Happiness After Hurting

Rebuilding and Healing Your Life After Divorce

Gessy Martinez, LPC, LCDC, NCC

This book is designed to provide helpful information on the subjects discussed. This book is not meant to be used to diagnose or treat any medical or mental health condition. For diagnosis or treatment of any medical problem, consult your own medical or mental health professional. The publisher and author are not responsible for any state that may require medical supervision and are not liable for any damages or negative consequences from any treatment, action, application or preparation, to any person reading or following the information in this book.

Neither the publisher nor the individual author(s) shall be liable for any physical, psychological, emotional, financial, or commercial damages, including, but not limited to, special, incidental, consequential, or other damages. Resources are provided for informational purposes only and do not constitute an endorsement of any websites or resources. Readers should be aware that the websites and resource contact information listed in this book may change.

Although I am a licensed professional counselor, I am not your counselor. Reading this book does not create a patient-client relationship between us. This book should not be used as a substitute for mental health services of a competent mental health professional credentialed and authorized to practice in your state or country.

This publication is prohibited from reproduction, stored in a retrieval system, or transmitted in whole or in part, in any form or by any means, electronic, mechanical, photocopying, recording, or otherwise without prior written permission of Aspire and Reach for More, LLC.

Copyright © 2011, 2016, 2017, 2019, 2021 Gessy Martinez
Publisher: Aspire and Reach for More, LLC.

Austin, Texas

All rights reserved.

ISBN:
978-0-9746939-9-6

Library of Congress Control Number: 2019934795

DEDICATION

This book is dedicated to everyone who had to rebuild through the pain of divorce, to my source of strength, faith, and hope in God. My husband and children who give me the encouragement, drive, and support to follow my dream and serve others. To all the courageous people who struggle and keep going, despite the difficulty, and rise above the circumstances to dream, build and learn to laugh again. This book is about you and for you. It doesn't matter what stage you are in right now; things can and will get better.

Contents

Introduction: 6
The End! 8
Pre-Divorce 12
Should I get divorced? 12
When is it time to divorce? 22
What mistakes should I avoid? 27
Why does this feel like someone died? 38
What should I expect? 42
Why me? 48
Why did they cheat? 50
Why did I not see this coming? 56
How do I let go of my ex? 62
When do I let go of the other person? 68
How do I stop being angry all the time? 71
Where did this anger and anxiety come from? 75
Why do I want them back, is this normal? 81
Can I make it alone? 84
How do I rediscover my voice, my life? 87
How to I explain what happened? 90
Why do I feel worst after? 93
How do I stay hopeful? 98
Where do I start? 102
How do I deal with loneliness? 107
How do I avoid making a mistake? 111

5 / Happiness After Hurting

How do I deal with the fear? 116
How do I stop being anxious? 120
How do I forgive? 124
How do I stop thinking about revenge? 128
How do I stop being triggered? 132
How do I protect myself emotionally? 136
How do I trust again? 140
How do I avoid repeating relationship mistakes? 144
How did I lose a spouse and pick up a habit? 147
Will my finances recover? 151
Will the kids/family forgive me? 154
Am I too old to start again? 158
How can I tell if things are getting better? 161
What's next for me? 163

Introduction:

Just Us Exes...

Everyone gets married hoping it will last; this is for guidance and hope when the marriage doesn't survive. When staying together becomes dangerous or toxic. If working out the problem seems impossible, divorce appears to be the only option; separating becomes the only available tool to resolve the pain of betrayal, disappointment, or abandonment. After working through a divorce, I wrote this book for you, a painful process that I am familiar with both professionally and personally. There was a time when my world was a mess, and the pain in my heart was so great. This time was difficult and uncertain, not knowing where to begin picking up the pieces. Those were the times I needed someone to come alongside to instruct and coach me. Someone to teach how to go through the hills and valleys, the silent days and years, and everything in between. I needed warning of the dark alleys and the confusing streets that I would have to navigate, all while carrying a load seemingly too heavy to bear. I lived back then with the feeling that everyone could see my shame. I was fortunate to have friends and professionals working with me through the process. This experience and passion for helping others led me to get the training necessary to help others skillfully.

I hope that the lessons shared in this book from others going through this process will encourage you in your journey. You will find insights from working with clients who have gone through a divorce and successfully found healing, and you can be confident that you are not alone. There are many people with similar stories and relateable experiences. There are some steps you must take. Emotions you need to release and truths to embrace. Explore the tools and actively answer the questions to help you successfully navigate this time in your life.

This book takes you through three parts of the healing process. We will begin with where you are and take you through the steps leading to where you want to be. Take your time and come back to the parts you find difficult. There are questions in this book that walk you through the process. Each person will experience divorce differently. For some, the pain is before the legal process starts; for some, it's during the legal process, and for others, it's years after the judge signs the final divorce decree. You are in charge of your healing process; use this book in stages you find yourself. When you complete it all, you will find some of the insights learned will cross over to other areas of your life beyond divorce.

Compassionately Yours,

Gessy Martinez

Section 1

The End!

9 / Happiness After Hurting

Life right now may seem to echo these two words, The End. Like a movie, it's over too soon; you still have questions, thoughts, feelings left unexpressed, but it's over. You are alone sitting in the dark, in a space that seems so big; it's cold, it is becoming a dark, lonely night for you, and your soul is crying, wailing, and empty. The silence in your home deafens you. You fear getting up from this place because you don't know where to go or what to do next. You are ashamed, sore, feeling discarded, and anxious. Unlike in the movies, you are playing the lead, supporting characters, and several other roles, the scenes will not end when you need a break, you cannot direct the other actors, and there is no happy ending, just yet.

Divorce is the end of one relationship but the redefining of another. You are discovering the difference between who you have become and who you are at the core. Divorce is the end of a drama and the beginning of a story. Revival and renewal can become the main subject of your new narrative.

There is so much tension in the divorce process because many people try to give advice. The goal, in the end, should be to try to have a peaceful separation. Utilize your lawyer to protect your rights and property. Be careful when everything is over, to have a bridge for building the future. If you have children together when the dust settles, you will have to find a way to have peace while protecting the children from further pain.

Adjust your expectations!

Be prepared that divorce may take years and more money than you anticipated. The divorce length and depth will depend on several factors. Those factors are your ex-spouse and the legal requirements of the judicial system. There are no absolutes, and no two divorces are exactly alike. The advice can be helpful. Legal guidance is necessary; nevertheless, in the end, no one can guarantee specific outcomes. There are several ways to divorce, using mediation, litigation, or a simple cooperative agreement.

If you have children in common before you divorce, the marriage ending is not always the end of the arguments. The separation may bring on a new set of problems you did not anticipate and complicate all relationships involved. Your children may be watching the family members grow instead of shrinking. Your ex-spouse in a new relationship comes with an increased number of family connections. The holidays can become more complicated, contentious, or require a lot of pre-planning conversations. The after-divorce repairs and residue will require your time and emotional energy. The end is not always the end; it is the beginning of a different phase.

Grief and divorce have a lot in common: both can bring on a tremendous amount of pain, shock, guilt, shame, and loneliness. Loss of a loved one or the loss of marriage will change and challenge the plans you had for your future. The challenge of learning to go forward with a different goal and without someone you thought would be a friend or partner for life.

11 / Happiness After Hurting

You are aware things will never be the same again, feeling you are not ready for what comes next. Some worries, doubts, and fears come up:

- Can I pay the bills alone?
- How much is the divorce going to cost?
- What about shared things in joint accounts and investments?
- How are we going to share custody of our children?
- Can I move out of state?
- How is this divorce going to impact my job, my reputation, my extended family?
- Do I have the emotional energy left to deal with this?
- How long is the divorce process going to take?

There are situations or pre-existing circumstances that can further complicate the divorce. If you or your partner are dealing with health issues, your health insurance could be jeopardized if you separate now. If a partner is incarcerated, overseas, or has mental health issues, this can delay the divorce process or require extra steps before finalizing the divorce.

How can you prepare for dealing with the situation

What are some of the unique situations that could complicate your divorce?

Pre-Divorce

Should I get divorced?

13 / Happiness After Hurting

Examine the relationship and ask the three following questions as you weigh your options. Can this relationship be repaired? Are both parties willing to work on restoring the marriage? What does an improved relationship look like daily interactions?

The first question: can this relationship be repaired? Asking this question examines the core of the problem in the marriage. What if the problem is an affair? Can it bounce back from the loss of trust, intimacy, and lies? One person has betrayed the marriage bed's sacredness and intimate space shared with their partner by inviting someone else in. It is leading to broken faith in each other and a lack of trust. Understanding this makes it difficult to forgive, forget, and start over. The intimacy and trust violation causes the affair to be more than just a mistake or physical act. Depending on how sacred your partner views marriage values such as privacy, loyalty, and intimacy, these factors make an affair more devasting or traumatizing to a relationship.

Privacy: Once a partner begins to cheat, the confidentiality that was protected is now open. The other party in the affair has access to your husband or wife. If they are aware of the marriage, they know more about the spouse than the spouse knows about them. Likely, the cheating partner told information about the discontent, disappointments, or needs not met. They are making the non-cheating spouse vulnerable to scrutiny and comparison without their knowledge.

Loyalty: This is a value many people have and wear as a badge of honor. If you ask that person what values they cherish in a friend or partner, and the first thing they say is loyalty, you know this is important. The betrayal of that loyalty impacts their ability to trust and leaves them feeling like "I can't trust anyone." They are asking questions like, "can I trust you to be there for me?" Your partner's affair could be interpreted as "I am not valuable enough for you to get your loyalty." Whether this statement is true, the actions, hurt, and unfaithfulness are causing them to not be fair and balanced in their thinking.

Intimacy: It is a powerful experience to be naked emotionally and physically with another person. The sanctity of intimate moments expected in a marriage relationship must be protected. It is painful when someone you care about shares intimacy with another person who has not earned that right. They have betrayed the connection achieved through vows, time, shared love, and experiences.
They have exposed the proud and not so proud parts of their bodies, lives, and emotions. It creates a shared experience making thoughts of jealousy, confusion, and inadequacy play havoc in the mind, worsening the act's pain.

In a relationship torn apart by unfaithfulness, addressing the issues at its heart can be a starting point for repairing the relationship. The process will not be easy or quick, learning the truth about the unfaithfulness level.

Unfaithfulness factors such as how many relationships and if anything, such as a child, disease, or legal troubles resulted from the affair, will make repairing the relationship even more difficult.

The next question: are both parties willing to work on repairing the relationship?

1. Are both parties ready to listen and honor the other's opinion? Can this take place without the exchanges turning into verbal disputes, heated arguments, or stalemates? Becoming prepared to listen implies that both people are at a place where they see the possible benefit of hearing the other side of the story. Learning from your partner possible reasons why the relationship has gone wrong or affections changed can trigger defensiveness.

2. Have you done the work to prepare emotionally for what you might hear and learn about your partner about the relationship? When you see your partner, feelings of pain, disgust, hurt, or shame are intense, indicating you are not ready. Emotionally prepare to be in a state where listening and hearing past the pain is possible. In relationships where one person responds with anger and aggression in difficult conversations, more work needs to be done. Intense feelings indicate it will take more time before sitting down to negotiate or talk about the future because the present situation is unsafe.

Emotional and physical safety is a priority before engaging in tough talks. Give yourself and your partner the time to prepare, get help, and ensure it's safe for both parties.

3. Can you participate in conversations that will take time? Expect that communication and feelings may not be resolved until many visits. Are you preparing for a possible need for a neutral third party such as a therapist to help you move through? Many people want quick fixes to lessen their pain. Some will go into these meetings impatient to know all and move on as soon as possible. The challenge with this approach is the deep work of healing, understanding, and communication is not quick. It does not consider or allow your partner to engage in a meaningful way if you are rushing to get to a solution.

4. Do both parties have the ability or willingness to be fair? If you have been the partner that gives in during arguments and hides your discontent, this may not be the time to engage. For this to work and move the relationship forward, both parties' needs must be addressed. Safe boundaries for communication and emotional sharing to ensure protection for both in the future must be decided.

The next question is: what does an improved relationship look like if we stay together? When it seems like everything has gone wrong, the connection is self-destructing; answering this question can be challenging.

17 / Happiness After Hurting

The first response is just to stop the unraveling of the relationship. The rush to take care of the emergencies or clean up the mess has taken over your ability to imagine a better relationship. Right now, the need to stop arguments, make peace, or stop the divorce proceeding and consequences have fogged up you're thinking. *Can this relationship be repaired, and what would that look like if you woke up and circumstances changed tomorrow?*

_____

_____

_____

_____

A clear and simple answer is hard to define due to the muddiness and mess of shattered trust. Once the hurt feelings and disappointment are the only things you can see, taking the time to dream again is difficult. The possibilities of a repaired and healthy relationship seem so far removed. Asking the questions: If the problem, for example, infidelity, health or emotional stressors, financial problems, dissatisfaction, contempt was gone, could this marriage be saved? Peace, love, and intimacy, what do they look like in a repaired marriage? What would be enough to grow going forward?

It is hard to see how good the relationship can be after months or years of dealing with the pain. The future imagined can help clarify your expectations and desires. If you are having difficulty conceiving a different life without your spouse, that is normal and expected.

Before pulling the plug on your friendship and future, answer the question, what do I want? What do I need? Are there other ways to get to a resolution? Imagine everything fixed: what would be different in the relationship? Can the answer help bring clarity? Yes. Getting a vision of the marriage without the existing problems will help determine if something is worth saving. It will help you to set a goal for the change you want to see.

The next step to explore is what does my partner wants from the marriage? What have they asked me to change, improve, or stop doing? What needs to change?

Is this a problem or a personality issue? Would both of us changing be enough to save our marriage? Has the problem between us grown to the point of no return, or is communication too broken to repair? This exercise places your desire and needs at the forefront of your mind while you weigh the possibilities.

Your marriage is unique; the decision of whether to stay in and try to work out the issues needs the thoughtfulness you are giving. Allow yourself the time and mental energy required, because the stress can cloud your ability to make a clear decision. It will take time to figure out what is the best way to move forward. Your thoughts and emotions in the moment of anger or sadness will leave you biased towards either going or staying. Pause before you decide.

Before making this lasting and emotion-filled decision, keep exploring, asking questions, and seeking clarity. Protect this critical decision from friends or family influences that may have a vested interest in your relationship's failure or repair. An example of this is pressure from friends who don't like your spouse, or a parent that micromanages gives unsolicited advice.

If you feel like the emotions or pressure of deciding are becoming more than you can handle, explore seeking counseling from a licensed professional. Getting help from a neutral, third-party professional as you go through the process can help you learn how to manage emotions and expectations.

You can separate fact from fiction. This decision about your future is significant, don't let others hurry or pressure you into it.

You have several internal questions to resolve that will allow the divorce to proceed healthily:

- Is there a dispute over the children before divorce?
- Are you struggling with bouts of anger and unable to talk to or be around your ex-spouse without an intense physical or emotional reaction?
- Is a rigid spiritual or cultural belief making it challenging to leave a toxic or unhealthy marriage?

- Have you become sad and anxious, having feelings of hopelessness lasting for more than a few hours or several days?

- Are you experiencing a loss of interest in things you used to care about, low energy, trouble focusing, or problems sleeping?

- Were you dependent on your ex-spouse to pay the bills, care for the children, or do things that you now feel unsure that you can handle by yourself?

- Is the thought of taking on these tasks causing you high anxiety, feelings of vulnerability, or loss of confidence?

- Has the separation come suddenly without any provocation or preparation, leaving you feeling overwhelmed?

- Is this your second divorce or part of a failed relationships series, and it's left you with more questions and added emotional pain?

- Are you safe from emotional abuse if you stay in this relationship? Will your partner keep bringing up the past if you remain in the marriage.

Answering yes to any of the above questions is an indicator your divorce will be emotionally complicated. If you are trying to determine if you need the help of a therapist, the questions above should lead you to seek out help.

21 / Happiness After Hurting

When dealing with depression, stress, children, past failures, or emotional/physical abuse, additional help is needed.

Pre-Divorce

When is it time to divorce?

23 / Happiness After Hurting

The decision to stay in a marriage or leave is never easy or perfectly timed. There are many things to consider before deciding. You have to check your emotional pulse before deciding to divorce. Having some rules will help bring protection and balance into determining if you should stay married or get a divorce. The number one rule is not to decide under duress or while feeling unsure, anxious, panicked.

What is duress? Duress is a legal term defined as "unlawful pressure exerted upon a person to coerce that person to perform an act that he or she ordinarily would not perform." Feeling you must decide to get divorced today, tomorrow, next month because your partner is asking for a divorce. An example of duress is other people pressuring you to get divorced. Being manipulated by someone using money, emotions, or power to push you into getting divorced or signing the paperwork is duress.

Other times to not make a final decision would be when your spouse has just stirred the emotional waters. When your spouse calls or visits often to provoke you to respond. They throw around hurtful words like rocks into still water, saying things like "this is why I left," or "you are a terrible parent." Emotional waters with intense waves of frustration and fear by saying accusing statements or engaging in acts to get you to respond. Avoid deciding when hit with verbal statements meant to cause pain or actions intended to provoke and confuse you.

When emotionally depleted, consider waiting to make a long-term decision. Emotional fatigue can lead you to say yes when you mean no. It can leave you too tired to ask for fair terms, feeling of wanting an argument to end. Desiring relief from the current situation can lead you to compromise. When dealing with emotional fatigue, give yourself time to be in a balanced and healthy frame of mind before deciding.

Conduct a review of the marriage before making a decision. One way to look at the relationship more objectively is to start with a marriage timeline. Write down the good days, events, memories, challenging days, and negative experiences when building this timeline. Also, add stress that impacted your marriage during the life of the relationship. Marriage strain can come from many areas such as work, health issues, loss or death of a loved one, addiction, and unfaithfulness. This timeline will help get a balanced view of your marriage. You examine your relationship as a whole, not just the difficult time you are in now.

Decision paralysis is likely to happen. Divorce is an important and challenging process; therefore, you will feel uncertain several times before feeling sure about going forward and separating. Some of this will come from feeling uncertain because doubt has snuck into your mind. When your marriage is failing, that will impact your self-confidence. Lack of confidence is why it's hard to decide out of fear you will make the wrong one.

Being emotionally vulnerable, you may experience uncertainty, lack of hope, and being stuck, which leads to deciding to do nothing.

Deciding when to get divorced will hit another roadblock—figuring out the best time of year, season, or after a big event such as the children graduating. You will start and stop if you are working on repairing the relationship while the divorce papers are submitted. It may be more helpful to work on counseling and determine if the marriage could be restored before filing. Both parties can focus on repair rather than have their emotional energy and focus split between two agendas.

There are three things to consider; 1) admitting mistakes, 2) taking responsibility, and 3) allowing yourself to not be on a clock. These are three ways to make the decision easier, rational, and less intense. Admitting mistakes allows humility and empathy to come into the process of deciding whether to stay in the relationship or separate. When you can see your contributions, this turns the emotional meter down and allows essential information to come through.

Taking responsibility will allow your partner to believe you are sincere in wanting change or a good outcome. Owning your part in the marriage problems is the beginning of rebuilding trust in the relationship. Your willingness to take responsibility for your actions can help the other person consider doing the same thing. Taking responsibility instead of throwing blame back and forth is a healthier form of communication before deciding to divorce.

You have a greater chance when the divorce process starts to be less contentious because your partner does not feel like they are the only guilty party in the marriage's failure.

Permit yourself not to be on a divorce clock. Should someone outside the relationship get to tell you when and how to divorce? You are the second half of the relationship and deserve not to be rushed through the decision by anyone. If you need more time, speak to your spouse, and negotiate for this. Don't let fear or the other person hurry to close the chapter or pressure you to make decisions you are not ready to process. Slowing down is not a license to take years to decide or draw out the process, yet it is essential to let your spouse and others know if you need time. If you do not ask or express the need for more time, how will they know you need it? Don't regret slowing down the process if you have the option.

Pre-Divorce

What mistakes should I avoid?

If you have decided that divorce is the direction you are going, there are some mistakes you want to avoid to protect yourself emotionally during the process. Emotional protection begins with building new habits and stopping old habits that can hurt your emotions and self-confidence. Protecting yourself from being left with paralyzing anger, shame, or fear. Here are some of the common problems experienced.

Not shielding yourself from social media. Social media is a great communication tool that becomes a weapon of destruction, spying, and comparison if you don't limit it quickly. The feelings in many divorces intensify because of the cheap shots taken over social media; the mean comments, insults, flaunting of success, minimizing of events, and highlighting of failures. Reading, monitoring, or engaging in your spouse's social media can add to hurt feelings, jealousy, and insecurities you are struggling with as you separate. Social media is a window to your emotions from a distance. You can open your feelings to being pulled and tested by engaging in social media disputes and comparisons.

Leaving open doors into your space. When you leave openings or things uncovered, your ex could get into your life and do some severe damage financially and emotionally. A lawyer might advise you to open individual bank accounts and then close joint accounts as one way to protect yourself financially.

This action prevents you from waking up one morning and finding your accounts are locked, and money is not accessible because your spouse has closed or emptied the accounts. The emotional damage done in these scenarios is the feeling of abandonment, betrayal, and hopelessness from being left without any way to pay your bills or get to work.

Limiting yourself to one way of working. "The only way, the right way, is my way." When you are considering divorce, it may seem that there is only one way to get a divorce and one outcome, thinking, "we separate, I keep my stuff and get what I earned. The kids stay with me, of course." The result is not guaranteed to benefit you in a divorce. You may expect to get the kids primarily right after the divorce, but the truth is, the kids may not live with you until five or ten years after the divorce. Did you clench your teeth or feel a sense of resentment when you read that last line? Open up to the possibility of a different ending from the one you want.

Your ex-spouse will have a say in this negotiation or direct the outcome. Consider the many different makeups of a family, including alternative schedules, sharing time, and placing the children's needs above both parents' needs. Consider alternative outcomes to emotionally protect you from the uncertain and problematic results of custody or alimony hearings.

Refusing to see the alternatives. Often in divorce and custody proceedings, both parties' unwillingness to see choices causes tremendous pain to the children and others in the family, even more than the adults divorcing. When children and loved ones are involved, consider reframing the need to win to build a loving future insulating the children. What is the most loving situation for my children, considering their personalities, health, and education needs? Even if this means the children are not with me much of the time? What living situation will give my children a stable launching pad for success? Where is the best place for what they want and need?

Suppose you make the most money and provide kids with the best material goods but are never home, traveling often and hiring a babysitter to care for the children most of the time, but your ex-spouse works a flexible job and can spend more time with them. The person not traveling can be the best scenario for physical custody if all other factors are equal and benefit the children.

A liberal, flexible visitation for the parent who travels often may be the best outcome. Remember being a great parent is not about outdoing the other parent; it's not about the amount of time but also the quality of time with your child. Great parents make their children feel loved, understood, supported, and so much more; you can be an outstanding parent, full-time, part-time, and with alternative schedules. Be open to a different arrangement, fluid outcomes, and putting the children first.

Keeping the house but losing your peace of mind. You are idolizing an object by holding on and giving it more value than your wellbeing.

We can easily let something material take on such significance, holding you back from moving forward in your life. Some divorces have made a house, car, or item so valuable the ex-partners spend years and thousands of dollars fighting over the thing. What is the motive you are operating under, holding on to the object? Some people will hold on to the house out of revenge, making the other partner pay as a form of emotional or financial punishment. Others hold on to the house because of fear, "where will I go? I can't ever have something like this again." Holding on out of hope, "this is the last thing I have from our marriage, from the children's memory, I don't want to let it go." If you step away from the sentiment and permit yourself to let it go in exchange for the freedom and peace you are about to gain.

The house could be amazing, but after living in misery in the house and fighting almost to the point of exhaustion or breakdown, is it worth it? You tell yourself, "I want the house for the kids." If all your energy, joy, and peace is gone from fighting for the house year after year, how can the kids enjoy it? What do you do when they grow up and move out. The memories they have of the house are frustrated parents back and forth to court, a parent unable to enjoy time with the children because they live afraid.

Afraid your ex will come and take the house, fearful of not being able to pay the mortgage or the taxes. Clarify, is your fight for the home about winning or about peace?

Allowing anger to become the only emotion expressed. Coming up, you will find a chapter on handling anger; this is a teaser to that chapter. When in conflict with someone you once loved, your rage can flare out of control. Under the feelings of frustration are a long list of other emotions. There can be feelings of sadness, deception, embarrassment, shame, jealousy, desertion, rejection, and much more. Anger, one of the strongest emotions, is used to mask more complex feelings. Anger comes up when you least want or expect it. Small reminders, significant events, and just the sight of your ex can send you straight into frustration mode.

Do not let anger cause you to react; give yourself a mental pause button when the feelings of anger arise. One physical way to reduce anger is to take a walk, even if it's just to the restroom, to give yourself time to take a breath, walk out the energy building in your body, and get space from the problem. The phone does not come with you on your walk because it's an access point to get you in trouble when you are angry. Anger in divorce is expensive, the consequences, the lawyers intervening, the evidence left to use against you. Anger can start as a small offense and result in a full-blown police-involved war of words, blame, or harmful actions.

Using your children and loved ones as weapons, pawns, or allies in the war. Avoid doing damage by involving your children or your family in inappropriate conversations about your ex-spouse. There is a temptation to defend yourself or get others to understand, sympathize, or take sides when in pain. Sharing the hurt and frustration you feel can, although legitimate, cause deep scars and harm to your children. It can bring about awkward moments for your family, who may continue to interact with your ex-spouse long after the divorce. Children don't want to take sides and should not because even if they seem on your side now, the things shared about their parents can be turned on you later when they can truly express how painful feeling forced to choose sides was.

Your children are smarter and more in tune than you give them credit for at their age. They need to be able to co-exist and love both parents equally. They are emotional sponges, and the toxic words about the other parent can leave them feeling insecure, unsafe, and not trusting you or the other parent. The emotional stress and uncertainty you feel going through a divorce with all the maturity and emotional capacity you have can be overwhelming and debilitating. Imagine how harmful this is for a child without emotional maturity taking even a portion of the complex emotions you are dealing with right now.

Remaining in denial about the marriage ending. As you continue this journey, there will be days when the circumstances become emotionally overwhelming. How do you deal with those feelings? Your mind will go into protection mode and look for a defense mechanism that helps you cope with the feelings, thoughts, mental and physical stress associated with the separation.

Defense mechanisms are unconscious actions and ideas that provide a protective barrier or shield during intense emotion, perceived threats, and guilt.

One of the defense mechanisms is denial. When you are in denial, the protection provided is time, a delay of the pain you think comes from the loss. Denial can look like avoiding the paperwork, not opening the mail, and wearing the wedding ring long after the divorce is final. Holding on, hoping your partner will have a change of heart when they are in a new relationship. You lie about the marriage doing well or say it's a temporary separation when your partner has moved out, looking for any sign, words, or gestures that make you believe the marriage is not over. Making excuses for your partner, saying that your relationship is unique, despite all the evidence that it is over.

Delaying the work you have to do because you are overwhelmed. One of the most common questions I hear clients asking is, "when will this be over?" They are not asking this question to get a hard date, but to know how long this pain and uncertainty will last.

The problem is really about the feeling they want to change, knowing when they will have a sense of peace, control, and experience love again. Every divorce is different, and getting a rigid timeline is impossible. The factors of people, relationships, and decisions have a lasting impact causing the timeline to vary. Don't wait till everything is over to begin to heal. Waiting to do the work of recovery is delaying an essential process and source of strength.

Don't wait till you fall to the bottom of the ocean to begin swimming up for air. Swim when you feel you are sinking, and get air before you need it.

Trust yourself more than you trust others. Many people want to advise you about what you should do, how to feel, react, or not react. Listen and sort through the external messages. Be sure to weigh the advice with what you want for your life. You have the most significant vote on how to move forward. The advice from the people close to you will range from the friend telling you to be healthy to the Wikipedia-informed lawyer friend directing your perfect response to every legal situation.

Your highly opinionated family member may be voting for your divorce to help you avoid pain. Despite the well-meaning friends and family, your divorce and healing process needs to be on your timetable when you are ready. This is where confidence in your choices and desires becomes very important; your friends and family will not live with your decision.

Divorce can shake you to the core of your soul and cause your mind to flood with questions. At some point in the process of the separation, you will have feelings of not being comfortable. Uncomfortable about the mixed emotions, having to make so many decisions without knowing if they are right. There are moments when you will feel helpless, unsure, and anxious.

At stake is something valuable to you; family, future, and reputation. Incidents will happen to make you feel insecure with your former spouse and others. Distrust will appear because you are cautious and don't want to make another mistake since this one left a great deal of hurt and shame. Learning to trust your decision-making will take time. Rebuilding your confidence comes one decision at a time. The decision to get married may have been the right decision at that time. You are the one who has the final say; trust yourself; it is part of your recovery process.

Start saving your money and living within your means. As you are considering whether to stay married or divorce, finances are a significant concern. Do not make the mistake of continuing to live a lifestyle that is more than you can support on your own. Don't count on a divorce settlement or spousal support to pay all your bills or meet your needs because it can be years before the divorce is final. In the end, you may not get what you expected for many reasons.

The expense of the divorce alone can take a large amount of the money you expected out of the final order or the amount you get monthly. The other danger of relying on your former spouse for financial support is being tied to them for the lifetime they are supporting you. This is not to say you are not entitled to the support, it is not to be stuck or hinged on the divorce outcome. The outcome can be full support, no support, or a fixed-income lifestyle; consider and plan for all the possibilities to remain prepared.

Pre-Divorce

Why does this feel like someone died?

Grief is the invisble elephant in the room, the thing no one talks about, the source of your tears, anger, and disappointment. When we think about grief, we associate it with the death of a living person or a pet. Divorce will cause you to feel the loss of your marriage, hopes, and past. The time, energy, shared resources, and memories will cause pain when it is taken away.

The death felt in divorce is the passing of hopes of life together, the loss of love, intimacy, and friendship. As you remember the good times, it will not make sense. You will miss the laughter, fun, sex, and security felt having a partner. Grieving in a marriage has all the emotional elements of loss, including shock, denial, anger, depression, and guilt.

Your recovery from the ending of your relationship begins with acknowledging your losses. Your ex leaving has cost you many things and has introduced the pain of loss into your life. Some of the losses will be easy to identify, while others will be revealed in time. When this happens, it will not matter how far you have come in your process the moment when another loss is shown, and the pain will feel fresh all over again.

The journey at this point will seem like for every step forward, life is knocking you two steps back. That will not be true; the discovery of another loss reveals the depth of the relational ties and how encompassing your relationship was.

Depending on the intensity, length of time, the involvement of children or loved ones, the depth of pain will reflect the relationship's depth and reach.

You will have to face and process each loss as it is revealed; this is key to accepting the loss and healing from it. Give yourself permission to grieve each loss as you grieve the relationship. Do not underestimate the impact that loss is having on your life. Allow healing to take place by acknowledging the loss.

With the end of your relationship, many losses occurred:

- Loss of your dream relationship and life together
- Loss of your status as a couple and a sense of belonging to a group
- Loss of the dual-income
- Loss of excitement, joy, someone to share with
- Loss of an intimate physical partner
- Loss of time and years invested
- Loss of reputation and other relationships
- Loss of confidence, trust, the hope of a future with someone
- Loss of control, predictability

Take time to come face to face with the emotions you are feeling towards your ex. If they betrayed you, also examine your thoughts and feelings towards the other party involved. The next activity will allow you to hear the thoughts of someone going through the divorce process and who was the victim of an affair.

41 / Happiness After Hurting

 She wrote both letters to express the thoughts she was having at the time and confront the feelings while providing a safe outlet to be truthful about the pain and anger she was feeling. As you read both letters, notice the feelings you identify with and create your own letter not to be sent to your ex or shared with others, solely as a form of release and expression of your emotions.

If you are asking the question, is it possible to put the marriage to rest peaceful? Yes. It will take a willingness to forgive and go through the process of grieving and allow healing to occur. Remember the most beautiful parts of the marriage, why you fell in love, and the memories you created. Honor the moments, experiences, and joy they brought into your life and that you gave to your partner. Admit the good in your partner. There is something in them that makes love possible. You were not a fool for falling in love, and you deserve love. You were brave, and it did not work out, not because you lacked courage.

Section 2

During Divorce

What should I expect?

Separation brings a wave of different emotions depending on where you are in the process. Expect your experience of divorce will be different from what people have told you. Your responses are unique; you may stay in one emotion for the entire time or bounce back and forth between various feelings. Below is a divorce timeline with emotions that may be experienced during those times:

Pre- Divorce Emotional Timeline

Before Filing	Divorce Petition Filed
Lack of communication	Uncertainty
Lack of intimacy	Overwhelmed
Disappointment	Anger
Mixed emotions certainty and uncertainty	Denial
	Embarrassed
Feeling hopeless about marriage	Tense
Impatient	Cautious
Unhappy	Thrilled
Restless	

© Gessy Martinez, 2019

During Divorce Emotional Timeline

Spouse Notification	Drafting Divorce Degree/ Mediation
Fear	Mystified
Betrayal	Frightened
Offended	Shame
Relief	Reserved
Spiteful	Victimized
Exposed	Discouraged
Puzzled	Detached
Let Down	Grateful
Rejection	
Careful	
Sympathetic	

This period will feel like a boomerang, somedays of these emotions are internal, and other days you will blame it on your ex. You will feel like you want to scream out loud, and other days like you are holding your breath. Releasing your emotions by talking with friends helps lower the intensity and decrease feelings of isolation.

Post Divorce Emotional Timeline

Establishing Custody	Present Case in Court	Finalizing Divorce
Afraid	Judged	Uncertain
Grieved	Concerned/ Nervous	Hopeful
Bitter	Apprehensive	Lonely
Privacy Violated	Alarmed	Curious
Abandoned	Insecure	Surprised
Prohibited	Petrified	Satisfied
Irritable	Frustrated	
Hopeful	Justified	

This stage can last the longest and have breaks in between emotions. When things are going well and you see progress, this period will feel freeing. When something disappoints you it may feel like you are stuck in this stage. Do not let discouragement set in; you will get through this; everything you see is not the final outcome.

Can you relate to these common reactions and thoughts during a Divorce?

- *I forget often, and I am having a hard time concentrating.*
- *I am lonely and sometimes find myself thinking about the good old days.*
- *I feel sick all the time.*
- *I am angry all the time; everything irritates me, little or big things, people bother me.*
- *I am anxious more than ever.*
- *I cry all the time, and I don't always know why.*
- *My mind will not turn off, always thinking about what will happen next, what my ex might do.*
- *I can't sleep, and I am not eating.*
- *I try and keep it together all day long and get home and fall apart with no energy left.*
- *I have pain in parts of my body I never had before, and the doctor can't figure*
- *I want to move on now, but my ex is dragging this out.*
- *Why is this so painful, and when does the pain end?*
- *I am trying to maintain control, but I feel so out of control.*

All these thoughts can occur hourly, daily and for weeks. If you can relate to any of these thoughts, it signals how much the divorce process impacts your mind, emotion, and physical well-being, and it may be time to get help.

Are you doing any of these things to cope with the stress?

- *I am dating someone I don't care about as a distraction, but it's not working.*
- *I work to forget, by the time the day is over I don't have any energy to think about the divorce.*
- *I'm regularly eating more and more, and the weight is piling on.*
- *I always sleepy, my emotions are overwhelming and make me tired all the time.*
- *I am busy all the time, I am so involved in my kids activities to keep from thinking about this.*
- *I moved in with my family and hide away from everyone else. I am not leaving my room unless I have to.*
- *I started drinking on weekends to sleep or not feel the emotions, but now I drink every night.*
- *I read every book I own twice, and when the story ends, I dread it, because I don't like the reality I am in right now.*

These are unhealthy examples of how other people get through the days, weeks, and season of a divorce. Coping with stress is a matter of survival; seeking healthy ways to manage is the goal for long-term mental and emotional wellness. You will have many questions in your mind, and they will take over your thoughts if we do not put them to rest with truth and understanding.

During Divorce

Why me?

The why me question – affairs happened to many people, as well-known as Hillary Clinton, Wendy Williams, Jennifer Garner, Dennis Quaid, dealt with cheating scandals. Not everyone cheats; unfaithfulness is not due to what you have or don't have; it can impact any relationship that does not guard against it. Infidelity affects all walks of life, starting with the White House to the neighbor next door.

Politicians, businessmen/women, military leaders, pastors, neighbors next door, and ordinary and extraordinary people have been exposed for cheating. The common thread is their humanity, people with weaknesses and flaws who gave in to the temptation and risked everything for momentary pleasures. They allowed the weakness of the flesh, the lust of the eye, and pride combined to result in an affair. When your partner betrayed your trust after making a vow, it created a wound. Instead of "why me, what did I do wrong,"; ask, "why did they choose to give in to temptation?". Cheating involves choice, and your partner owns the responsibility for engaging in the affair.

Stop blaming yourself, constantly going over details, trying to figure out why you, why now, why this, will lead to more anger, frustration, and anxiousness. The next chapter will offer insight into some reasons people cheat. Right now, focus on you are not to blame, and your partner chose more about meeting their needs than about hurting you.

During Divorce

Why did they cheat?

Having an affair was simple. Why they choose to cheat is more complicated. For some men and women, it may be about the following:

Opportunity and Curiosity – the woman or man was available, willing, and without thought, they indulged in the risk, pleasure, and what seemed like a dare. The mentality is "I think I can get away with it," "I won't get caught, and I am just having fun." We were drinking, got carried away, and it happened; some affairs are just that quick and superficial. The curious part of this is a desire for a new experience, to spice up their life. The individual has entertained thoughts and fantasies that push them in the direction of the behavior.

Loneliness: They are married, settled in, bored, and not valued, understood, or sought after by their spouse. Their ego needed a boost, and they desired another's attention without any strings, demands, or history attached. They had the nagging question of "do I still have it?" The attention says, "yeah, you have it." Loneliness can start with emotional neglect and, over time, move to physical neglect deepening the divide in the marriage. The idea of becoming lonely inside of a marriage is not the fault of one person. There is a point where emotional intimacy is lost; this can happen because the couple becomes so busy doing the business of marriage, they forget to have fun. The couple stops being friends, allowing parenting to take over the marriage. When the work of the marriage overtakes joy and pleasure, the marriage can suffer.

Entitlement: Some men think, "as long as I am taking care of the home and the kids, I am entitled to fool around. What she doesn't know she isn't hurt by, and I don't bring it to the house. I keep the two separate; I deserve some fun, someone to take care of me. It's equal; I take care of both the mistress and the wife, so why not ?". There are women who think, "to get my revenge, I am going to have an affair," the other rationalizing that takes place is "I'm not getting my needs met, one person can't handle me."

This type of thinking is egotistical. Some are bored with current monogamous sex life and want to "spice it up", they may have asked their partner to sleep with other people and when they did not get the answer they wanted, did it anyway.

Sexual Disorder: This is a highly controversial thought: if your partner has a pattern of participating in multiple affairs with known or anonymous people, excessive pornography, masturbation, or engagement in cyber-sex, these can be indicators of a bigger problem. There is the possibility your partner suffers from a mental health condition related to possible sex addiction or hypersexual disorder. Some people use sex as a coping mechanism for avoidance or relief from life stressors, depression, and anxiety. This does not take responsibility away from the individual for their behavior but may give a window into the cause or the impulses and help you understand why this person continues to make the same choices despite the consequences and the pain they cause.

Revenge: The way to guarantee one wrong decision will be made worse is to make another bad decision. If you wonder why revenge is listed under the reasons for cheating, it can be one of the excuses given for having an affair.

This reasoning is used in two ways:

1. The cheating spouse says, "you did not pay attention to me; you controlled the money and everything we did; I had no power, no say in this relationship." The cheating spouse is trying to get the attention of the other spouse.
2. "You cheated on me, and I have not forgotten; I wanted you to know what it feels like. I wanted you to hurt as much as I did when you had an affair."

As you read the two accounts above and think this does not sound logical, that is true. It does not make any sense to the rational mind; it is the illogical heart leading the decision. In both scenarios are some of the real reasons couples have given in studies when asked why they cheat. This is a small number of people who use revenge and anger as reasons. Both scenarios involve feeling neglected and making a decision to get the partner's attention. Equally, there is a desire to get one partner to listen to and acknowledge the other's pain.

Pain left unanswered and not cared for like a wound, where the bleeding continues because it was not tended and closed.

No one came and applied ointment to clean out the wound, therefore it got worse. Now the pain has spread all over, and it went from a cut that needed stitches to an injury that has infected. This neglect has caused rot, and the entire body part needs to go before the infection gets to the vital organs. How do you stop pain from getting unmanagble? Address the issue before it gets out of control, don't let pain grow into something that suffocates your marriage.

Avoidance, ignoring, and hoping are not solutions. Things will not get better unless you confront the problem. Be careful with this response because the temptation is to take the blame for the failure of the relationship. The nature of any relationship is that it involves two people. Do not take on the blame for someone else's decisions. Their reasons cannot place further blame or cause you more pain. Take responsibility for your part in the failed relationship and allow your partner to own their part despite the excuses or reasoning. Being in pain is not a license to hurt others. The unmet need and feelings of rejection leading to revenge should not become reasons for entering into a cycle of hurt where everyone becomes a victim, and your marriage is the casualty.

Why an affair? Affairs are devastating, and the repercussions are far-reaching. Once or over time, they can destroy families, damage careers, bring down governments, public fiqures and cause someone to question their faith.

Stop the madness in your head, trying to blame yourself for not doing something to prevent the affair. An affair is not about how the other person looks or how you look; it's about how they feel about themselves. Affairs are about unmet needs and looking for a way to get the need met. In the search for why your spouse cheats, you will run through your mind thinking of every possible reason. You losing weight, or getting breast or butt augmentation, will not change things. Changing the way you cook, getting a job, or staying home or could not have guaranteed that he would never cheat.

You can always do something to protect your relationship, improve communications, spice it up, and make it better. Still, it does not guarantee the relationship will be repaired. It is essential to know if someone is unhappy with themselves or has a history of sleeping around; there is little you can do to change this until they are ready to change their behavior.

During Divorce

Why did I not see this coming?

This question involves you figuring out where the missed opportunities were to fix what went wrong. It is also part of getting an answer and protecting yourself in the future from further harm. Below are some of the subtle and not subtle ways a marriage can begin to show signs of vulnerability. Your marriage was vulnerable to an affair long before the affair took place. Some of the opportunities exist because of one person and or both parties.

Silence: Issues began to creep up in the marriage and failed to be addressed. Over time silence has filled the space where conversations would have allowed healing to take place. Silence in a marriage that was once filled with communication and laughter is a sign there is trouble. Feelings such as being overwhelmed, fearful, unsure, and disrespected can lead to the other person going into silent mode. If silence was used in the family of origin to avoid difficult emotions, it is a learned way to avoid conflict, which will be used again in the marriage. Some also use silence to manipulate the other partner into showing they care or apologize even if they are unsure what to apologize for since it is unclear. This effort to gain power in the relationship undermines the possibility of change. Using silence to manipulate or win a reaction can confuse your spouse about engaging in the marriage again.

Your spouse apologized just to end the uncomfortable silence, and after speaking, they retreated emotionally each time. When your spouse retreats inward, and you make the assumption "all is well" because you are satisfied, this is a missed opportunity. If you are not talking, exchanging thoughts, feelings, and ideas, you are not communicating. If your partner is not speaking, you are not a mind reader and cannot extract what is playing in their head. In this case, the silence becomes a cover for the affair. Symptoms of a marriage in trouble can be seen through nonverbal acts and the silence that fills the room every time you are together. This can confirm the other person has given up or they are focused on another relationship.

Secrets: Why would a partner keep secrets?
1. Because they are not ready, to tell the truth and stop the negative behavior. Some people enjoy the thrill of getting away with things, outsmarting everyone, and maintaining two lives.
2. In too far, the feeling that too much has happened to bounce back. They are not sure when to tell the truth, because of fear of repercussion. In acts of selfishness, your partner seeks to avoid the pain of consequences and secretly hopes never to be found out when it comes to the true extent of what they are doing.
3. Lying and keeping secrets have become a way of interacting; the lines have blurred, and the habit has formed. The spouse with the secret is procrastinating over telling the truth, not revealing how many other people have become a part of this deceit.

Weaponized words are when conflict continues to grow in the marriage, and no one wants to back down. The disrespect increases with every exchange. A wide opening exists between both parties, and coming to a comprise and growing closer together becomes more difficult. There are landmines in the middle of the couple. The landmines are made up of words used to inflict pain. Comments are used to cause the other person to feel embarrassed, attacked, and frustrated. The power of positive words used in a daily relationship can create a healthy, supportive, loving atmosphere. If you are thinking, "I have not used weaponized or curse words towards my spouse," have you been critical in the marriage? Were you ever accused of belittling, nagging, blaming, or being critical of the things your spouse has done? It is not the type of words said that make it painful; it is a word, phrase, or criticism that specifically attacks your spouse's core, making this tool destructive.

When words are weaponized, it becomes exchanging hurt for hurt. This exchange of harmful, abusive language can serve as a distraction to the conversation that needs to take place. It can be demeaning, exploitative, toxic, and manipulative. Words that remind your partner of failures or expose a vulnerability can leave them feeling angry, confused, unloved, and betrayed. If the weaponized terms are being used against you at some point, you may become desensitized or completely shut down.

Silence, secrets, and weaponized words can be contributors to the demise of a marriage. These choices of relating to one another can result in several outcomes:

1. One partner feels exhausted every time they want to engage because the outcome is to feel emotionally and physically wiped out.
2. Further avoidance, working long hours or more than one job, visiting family more often, and staying for hours.
3. Another tactic is putting other priorities in front of the marriage, for example, immersion in the kids' lives, activities, and medical needs. This becomes a reason given not to have time to engage and work on complex emotions.
4. Becoming increasingly passive-aggressive in conversations and behaviors. Using body language to convey disgust, disapproval, and hostility.

Abandonment: You or your spouse have reached the point in the marriage where leaving emotionally seems like the most effortless way to cope. The legal definition of abandonment is when a spouse leaves a marriage (physically) without any desire or intent to return or continue with the marriage. It is possible to abandon the marriage without leaving home, participating in the children's care and daily tasks while emotionally being distant.

Neglect: This is when one partner or both get busy and involved in the activities of family life, and the relationship gets ignored.

They are busy earning money to be comfortable. The focus is on achieving the dream life and missing the heart of the marriage. Attention is set in one area that has allowed the relationship to lose love, time, and investment. Giving gifts has replaced spending time. Being busy has become a badge of honor, and staying home, doing nothing, and enjoying your spouse feels like a waste of time. Values have been turned upside down, where quality time with your spouse no longer feels valuable or productive. You began to look forward to vacations once a year to get a break.

Strategies such as silence, secrets, and weaponized words do not allow your spouse the ability to vocalize the hurt and process the problem. Everyone in the family has the right to talk and share without fear or a fight.

During Divorce

How do I let go of my ex?

Just for the Release – Letting Go Letter to Ex

You can begin the process by doing the following activity of writing a good-bye letter. This letter is not meant for sending, it is to release the emotions, hurt that are bottled inside. Providing words to your pain and releasing as much as needed. This practice will help you identify the hurt, lessons learned and how you will regain your freedom.

Dear Ex,

The day you came forth and finally said those words that seemed to be eating at you was the day you changed my life. As I listened to your excuses, reasoning, and harsh words, I looked into the face of a man who did not understand the fallout of the choice he was about to make. Inside my stomach turned, my knees were shaking, my heart was burning, and my anger rose. I could not hear your excuses over the thumping of my heart. The room felt like I was losing oxygen. I listened to a myriad of voices in my head, one saying, "Is this actually happening," the other saying "what did I do wrong?" The mother in me thought, "how do I protect the kids?" and "who else knows this is happening?", the fighter in me saying, " you son of a bitch."

I wanted to hurt you as much as you were hurting me. I wanted you gone, out of my face and life, for it to be like you never existed. I hated you for all you did to me. I hated myself for allowing you to continue in your lies, to think that you somehow were fooling me into believing that you were faithful or happy. You stood in front of me with your chest puffed out, proud of yourself for taking the manly stance and being brave enough to admit the cowardly deeds you have done, and all the while, I could see the bumbling coward that you truly were.

I hope your inflated ego and the lie of a life you created for yourself was enough to keep you going. Did it buffer you from the reality that was headed your way, the moment of truth that lay ahead? There is a moment that will find you sooner or later when you realize that I was the best thing that ever happened to you.

When it hits you that the grass is not greener over there and you acknowledge responsibility, do not leave because you have left. Wherever you go, you carry with you your issues, needs, and baggage. The wonderful prize of girlfriend you have found will soon inherit all that they have stolen away and much more. There is a surprise that lies in wait for the two of you; I hope that once again, your ego rises to buffer you from the pain that you will inflict on yourself, and share with her because you refuse to deal with habits you formed.

"You good for nothing. I wish a taste of what you have done to me would happen to you." These are just some of the thoughts I had as you stood smugly, trying to find words to make yourself feel better, letting me know that you waited out of courtesy to me to inform me. That you made sure things were taken care of first. Patting your ego and believing your own press while you turned me into an uncaring, unresponsive villain and husband neglector. I stopped being the woman of your dreams and became the headline of your nightmare when you decided that you wanted something new, something different. Nothing I did was good enough, or everything right in our lives became wrong because you needed a way out that still matched up with your image of yourself.

Sincerely,

A Woman Set Free

Pause: As you have read this letter from this fellow traveler, you may have added to this or thought as your emotions rose, "I would not have been so kind." There may be parts of this letter you identify with; you may think this was too harsh. What would your letter say? Get a pen and pad or keyboard and start your own release letter to the ex. Don't email or mail it; just write it for your own peace of mind.

We cannot heal until we are honest; denial only serves to perpetuate what already exists. Speak your truth in order to let it go. On the next page are prompts to help express your emotions and begin to sort out the complicated feelings and thoughts.

Your goodbye letter:

Dear_____,

The best part of our marriage was

_____

_____

The worst part of our marriage was

_____

_____

_____

_____

I expected

_____

_____

I received

_____

_____

Things began to go wrong when

_____

_____

I needed from you

_____

_____

You gave me

_____

_____

I wish for you

_____

_____

_____

If I could change one thing

_____

_____

During Divorce

When do I let go of the other person?

Just for the Release – Letting Go Letter to Mistress/Girlfriend

The following is one way to express unspoken pain while declaring your freedom. Create your release letter after reading, choosing to let the other person go from occupying space in your mind.

Dear Mistress,

I want to take the time to give you a gift that was not given to me before I took on the role of girlfriend, partner, wife. When I first learned about you, I was hurt, angry, and left wondering why and who. Why would someone want to go after someone else's man? Who is the kind of person he feels the need to hide, lie about, and sneak off with? What did I do wrong, and how could I have changed to keep him? Then it hit me that this is not about you or me. It is about a man who is unsettled in his role and in himself. A man who is running from issues needing to be resolved. A man hiding from becoming the man he should be in the arms and made up a life he now has with you.

Take care of yourself and do not do what I did in believing the lie, the lie that it would be forever, that he was loyal and devoted, and that I was the only one for him. You are looking at a man who knows the game, and once you make demands for the respect, love, and devotion you deserve; be careful because you will lose to the next woman who makes no demands and just takes whatever crumbs, lies, and little bits of affection she can get. I know you are hungry for affection, starved for a man to look at you and love you, but what you settled for in him is all fluff and no substance.

What you settled for was a man who will never truly be yours because he does not know who he is. You have settled for something stolen, which means it can never really belong to you. What you have not earned you cannot place a value on, or claim rights to. You have a loaner for a man, but do not worry. I don't want him back. Leaving was the best thing he ever did for me because it is how I became a grown, strong, and successful woman.

His leaving freed me to do what I did not think I could, to learn about and love myself. I am no longer chained to him. For being the jumping off board who made the process easier, I thank you. Take care of yourself and have an exit plan just in case history repeats itself, where you have the same script, but now you are in the lead role.

Sincerely,

A Free Woman.

What are you thoughts after reading this letter?

What would it take for you to forgive this person?

During Divorce

How do I stop being angry all the time?

There are days where the only constant will be the anger teeming up in your mind. Some anger will come from being disrespected, abandoned, rejected, lied to and forced to live a lie, from being placed in danger and stolen from, from the hurt caused to your children, loneliness, being forced to change without a say.

You will express some truths that you have held back in your anger and were afraid to admit. You will become angry with the mistress, your ex, your friends, and then yourself. Everyone will be to blame, and then you will be left wondering what you did wrong, how did you miss it, or why you allowed it. The anger will go from pissed off to raging, and you will feel like you are about to lose your mind.

You may wake up angry and go to bed angry. You can be emotionally stable one minute, then something is triggered and causes you to fly off the handle the next. The anger will seem justified, and your tactics for revenge will seem reasonable, but you will have to take control of it before it destroys everything that is left. Your anger towards your ex can be turned towards your children, family, and friends, and place those relationships in jeopardy. Your disappointment and anger towards yourself can become a depression if left ignored, unresolved, or untreated.

When we are angry, reason can be ignored; rash decisions are made, and people can get hurt. Anger is one emotion that can so overtake you that it becomes all-consuming of your time, energy, and strength. It is an enemy to your survival and can take control of your success.

Anger can be used as a tool because it works to some degree to get you what you want. The next questions are designed to explore why you would like to hold on to the anger and how this has worked for you. Becoming honest about how anger has worked for you is the first step in getting control and learning how to manage your anger.

How is your anger benefitting you?

_____

_____

_____

Why Should I Let the Anger Go?

If you do not let the anger go, it will consume you; anger is like wildfire inside of you. It will consume the spiritual oxygen needed to breathe freely, think, and live unencumbered. Your moments will be stolen by thoughts of vengeance, hatred, and feelings of irritation that will take over. This leaves you with the potential to go from being upset with the kids or something minor to fully fledged fury in 60 seconds or less. This inner and deep-seated anger will not be easy to pacify or soothe.

Unresolved anger is easily aggravated by the smallest action, memory, or other triggers. If you tell yourself you have it under control, be careful because you may not have had it thoroughly tested yet by the right set of circumstances or what is also known as the perfect storm.

Some triggers for anger when going through a divorce are:

- Rumors and lies being told about you
- Your ex spending the money in the joint account, spending child support money without a care
- Your ex is late to pick up the children or to an appointment
- Your ex won't sign divorce papers
- Your ex brings up a sensitive or private topic in front of strangers or lawyer
- Refuses to admit to an affair or an offense
- You are being wrongly accused
- Having to make something right with others or your children on behalf of your ex-spouse
- Your ex leaving your home a mess or things broken
- Your former in-laws being involved in child custody decisions
- Being given misleading or wrong info

Knowing your triggers and having a planned response or a way out can help you to begin controlling your anger and not letting the triggers set you on a path for a full-blown argument. The key to planning is to anticipate problems by identifying your triggers, examining your past behavior, and preparing alternative responses.

During Divorce

Where did this anger and anxiety come from?

Let's address the top two emotions that will follow you through the entire process of divorce. Anger and anxiety will be twin emotions that will show up on time and when you least expect it. If you currently struggle with either of these emotions, pay attention to the intensity levels during the divorce process and get professional help to prepare for and manage both feelings.

Examples of anger and anxiety at different stages in a divorce

When you learn the divorce is going to court

Angie thought she was over the anger until the day her doorbell rang. She was served with divorce papers, only to have her phone ring, and the ex remind her that he is no longer paying his share of the mortgage. She would have to sell the house and buy him out, and this call was followed by one from her employer later that day announcing the second round of job cuts in which her section stood to lose the most positions. By the end of the day, Angie was in a coffee shop line reviewing all that had transpired, and she boiled with rage at the nerve of everyone in her life, from the ex to the boss, just not giving a damn. She waited what seemed forever in line with her irritation building into seething anger, and when the server ignored her after several attempts to get her attention, Angie lost it. She went into a frenzy, shouting and shaking on the verge of tears, because her perfect storm hit and the tipping point of one more person's selfish act was enough for her to blow her top. Angie thought to herself, "Someone was going to get to hear my wrath, the girl in the coffee shop was just a victim of anger out of control and misdirected."

If you do not want this to be you, the anger must be dealt with and managed. It can no longer be used to protect you, you cannot use it to control others, and it cannot be held inside out of fear. You have a vested interest in getting the anger under control and getting it out of your life. Anger will kill everything; relationships, plans, energy, and hope, everything it comes in contact with in your life. As you develop new relationships, you will notice quickly that anger is unattractive, and next person does not want to deal with or have it directed at them. When misdirected anger is displayed around your children, they will think they are the reason for your anger. You cannot think straight or rationally when angry; it often causes us to say and do something regrettable.

Angie was both angry and anxious. The anxiety levels were so high that it fed into the anger. Anxiety about the divorce, the mortgage and the job. When answers and feeling more and more overwhelmed and then angry because of feeling helpless in dealing with so many problems.

When you learn your money has been taken or misused
You get a notice that you missed a car payment or your bank account is overdrawn. You are angry because your ex tried to destroy the comfortable life you built and damage your reputation. They obtained your credit information using secret means and proceeded on a shopping spree, buying things to support their new mate.

This kind of anger can begin with shock and feelings ranging from annoyance to intense frustration and feelings of vulnerability. Anxiety will show up in feeling vulnerable to being taken advantaged of again or in another area of your life.

Reading something over social media that seems to be about you

You read what is said about you and become aggravated, feeling powerless to defend yourself. The more you read, the more you become furious because the message leaves you feeling under attack. Your ex used their words, disclosing secrets and withholding facts to attack you at your weakest spot. The things said on their way out may have revealed some truths about the relationship you chose to ignore, something intimate you wanted to be left private and unknown that now you would have to contend with. Anxiety will come from thoughts of "what will they say next", or "who else is reading this", and "will they believe this stuff being said about me?".

When divorce papers are received

When the final divorce papers arrive, you will be faced with extreme feelings. From "is this really happening," "what did I do wrong, maybe I should wait, what if he comes back," "why am I paying for this crap, really?" "Thank God it's over," "What do I do now?" "I should have done this a long time ago. Why did I wait so long" "They will never get a dime!" To stop the rollercoaster of emotions, some people don't sign the papers under stress.

One way to turn this moment around may be as you sign exhale the old life, and when you turn it over, inhale your freedom. Freedom is priceless; it's a high-value item that is worth fighting and waiting for.

After the divorce is final and you see your ex again
There is no set time when you will be completely unmoved when you are in the room with your ex again. Anxiety and anger will linger in the middle of the exchange. The shared experiences and memories will also impact; the intensity and duration of the feelings will change. Over time some memories will take on new meanings, previously accepted things may appear different after some time, and revelation becomes a point of contention or pain. Other memories that were once negative may be brushed over. Some divorcees have shared different reactions to their ex six months or years after the divorce. A visit or encounter with your ex can leave you feeling anxious, and relieved when you think about your new life. On the other end of the spectrum, an encounter can bring up memories of a painful, bitter, backbiting divorce and cause feelings of anger to rise.

After the divorce, when you start dating again
You have begun to date again, and this person you found yourself interested in starts to do and say things that give you flashbacks of your ex. This is causing you to become guarded again and have some recurring feelings of anxiety and anger at yourself. The anger at yourself comes from feeling as if you should have seen this coming,

"I should have recognized this sooner" is the recurring thought in mind. Saying to yourself, "why do I keep attracting the same type of people? How come I was so blind?" These are unfair statements as you have attempted to rebuild trust and try to give meaningful relationships a chance.

It can be alarming after surviving the divorce process; any little signs that you would ever go through that level of intense heartbreak or pain is enough. Looking at the signs will make you want to turn on all your defenses and put a wall of resistance and protection between you and the possible offender. Once you recognize what is happening internally, it can cause anger, frustration, and resentment towards your ex-spouse to resurface.

During Divorce

Why do I want them back, is this normal?

This journey will have ugly moments filled with rage, hurt, anger, bitterness, and raw emotions. The background of all this will be the noise from others, their opinions. The overwhelmed thoughts in your mind are causing stress, and your emotions are stretched. The noise will overtake you in the morning before your feet hit the floor and surround you at night before your eyes close. Getting control will require letting yourself get quiet and gentleness take over when anger wants to lash out. Becoming quiet allows the strongest part of you to help regulate your mind, body, and spirit while preparing to make better decisions. Your first emotional reaction is usually not the right one, and until you can get control, the reaction may make the situation worse.

That silence drives you to and from home with the thickness of tension, anger, hurt, and pain in the air. You have the desire to scream out to your partner how upset you are, to let him know what you want and need. As human beings, there is a tendency to have moments where we find ourselves going backward in time. Going back towards the very things and people we said we were no longer going to be involved with.

The tendency is to have a temporary setback and then start rationalizing how this broken relationship could work. What if he changed? What if we got back together again? Maybe in a few years from now, he will realize the error of his ways and come back, and maybe then, if he has matured, we can reconcile. These wishful thinking scenarios mixed with desperation only work to hold you back from moving forward with your life and plans.

Do not get stuck in this sand trap that is waiting for the right moment to pull you down. Keep moving forward, refusing to look back or entertain what is not based in reality and can only serve to harm you.

If you find this difficult to do, then begin with all the things you will not miss that were negative in the relationship.

Things I Do Not Miss About the Relationship

Some examples are:

I will not miss living without love

I will not miss being in a home where I am not acknowledged

I will not miss being made to feel less than

I will not miss worrying about if he will come home or not

I will not miss feeling like I do not matter

I will not miss feeling unwanted

I will not miss being misunderstood

I will not miss being yelled at, bossed around, and bullied

I will not miss carrying the household burdens by myself and then being told I am not doing my share.

The list can be as long as you need it, to allow for release of emotions and reset when the pain of loss becomes overwheleming. This is a moment to allow the turth to return the emotions out of regret.

During Divorce

Can I make it alone?

During the divorce process, your ex will let you know out of anger or arrogance how they feel. Some of the comments will make you doubt you can be successful without them. You may hear quotes like "you can't make it without me". Do not believe the lie when they tell you can't make it without them. Their goal is to make you question yourself. Do not doubt yourself or let them plant seeds of insecurity in your mind. Your ex knows that you are scared, and will try and add to it with words that make you feel insecure and uncertain.

You can make it, your ex will have you believe you can't be successful without them, as if the sun, moon, and stars will cease to exist because they left. **You can and will succeed; it is a matter of fact that in you lies the grit, hunger, and survival skills to make it, and you will get through this.**

You are strong, resilient, and made to survive. This is just a test, and you can make it. There are many challenges in life, but none that are impossible. People are out there right now, proving the impossible is possible. Think of it this way, the people doing the impossible are flesh and blood humans who wake up just the way you do. Doing the impossible is not about not being scared; you can be afraid and choose to do it anyway. Doing the impossible is not about having all the answers or all the resources; we do not always have everything we need right when we need it; nevertheless, you can accomplish more than you think. If it's resources you lack, it may take some creativity to find them.

Being brave is not about feeling brave; it is a choice. A choice is made when the alternative is to hide, turn around, give up, or compromise; you are brave every day you fight to get your life back. You are courageous as you face the unknown of the future, and you keep moving forward. Be bold and get your life, your joy, your dreams back. Become who you were created to be before you found yourself in this situation. It is never too late to start over; you can make it without him.

Section 3

Post-Divorce

How do I rediscover my voice, my life?

Where am I? You have an opportunity that you will not have again. The ability to rediscover who you are and what you like, dislike, and want in your life now and years ahead. Rediscovering is an important step that you cannot miss or forget to do. Use this opportunity to get to know yourself and become clear about who you are, what you will accept and not tolerate. You have this chance to start over with a blank canvas, and on it, you can write the truth about who you are. You get to tell the world these are your values, beliefs, and the reality you live by. You are at the starting line of your new life.

As a woman looking at 50 in the front window of aging gracefully, I had to ask the question: Girl, you have a new decade ahead of you; what are you going to do with it? Here I am looking at 50 with a great sense of accomplishment, wonder, and a bit overwhelmed, knowing the decisions I make here at this time will impact my middle and silver years. Knowing I have even less time to do the things I dreamed about and less money to waste. The latitude I was once given due to age and inexperience does not exist anymore. The theme of this season is to maximize.

Every moment, every opportunity, and every relationship maximize. Time, health, and money in this decade are all precious. The work is in cultivating all three assets and not taking any for granted. How do I get more time? It's up to God how much time; it's up to me how effective the use of my time is. I need more health.

That is where my sacrifices lie, sacrifices made in eating right, working out faithfully five times a week. The lifestyle change is my key to more health. Pleasure seeking may have once ruled past decades but not this one; pleasure will lead to pain. When we are in our later years, the pain of discipline is rewarded, the lessons drawn from painful experiences in our lives become the teachers and guides on the road ahead.

Own your decade, your experiences, and your years. Own them like you have earned it, with interest. Taking charge begins with ownership, feeling free, and enjoying the power of deciding your course. When you remember that you control yourself, your actions, thoughts, and reactions, you can own what you choose to do or decide to refrain. Power and control feel great when you have them over yourself. It is dangerous when someone has them over you, so don't give them the opportunity or a window in. Keep what is yours, yours, and make them own what is theirs. Now move forward from asking, "where am I?' to asking yourself, "where do I want to go?"

Post-Divorce

How to I explain what happened?

Reframe to rediscover let the word divorce taking on a new meaning. Words are powerful; that's why I write to express emotions, thoughts, and ideas and help shape my future. The words I choose to believe will allow feelings, thoughts, and ideas to manifest into my reality. The mention of the word divorce for anyone who had to endure the pain and humiliation evokes memories we wish we could forget. Divorce marks the end of something in your life. Your memories become marked with a before the divorce and after the divorce timeline.

Take the word divorce and reframe it. When your ex has been gone for some time, and you wonder what I should do now? Should I divorce him or wait to see if it can be repaired if we get back together again? This is a very personal and individual decision that your friends and family should not push you to make until you are ready.

The task involved in getting a divorce may become as cumbersome and draining as the emotions stirred up. The shorter the marriage and less property between you, the quicker the administrative process to complete. If children are involved, their ages and medical or education needs will influence the length of time needed to work through the details of care, custody, visitation, and other issues.

Taking the word divorce and reframing the concept will help brace you for the impact and provide a hopeful expectation of the outcome. How can this happen? Look at divorce from the perspective of gaining your freedom back, not of being left.

It is viewing the breakup as leaving a dysfunctional, harmful, and not genuine relationship. For some, Divorce is a needed release from a relationship that needed repair that could not be done while you were entangled together.

Post-Divorce

Why do I feel worst after?

It is going to be difficult to move forward and face the challenges ahead. It is difficult being the one who is left, it is painful, and you have to acknowledge that. Your mind will race, thinking, "I do not want to do this. I do not feel like it! Why should I?" Yes, this is difficult; yes, it is painful. Everything in you will say, "I'd rather just stay here and sulk, stay and be angry," but you have to move forward. Why? No one should have the right to decide how your story should end but God. No one should be able to control your moods, causing you to live a life below God's best.

Acknowledge the true cost involved with a divorce; acknowledge it was shameful, but that will not become the word that describes you. Acknowledge, get it out of your system, and do not let it control your mind. Call it for what it was, then take it, and tell it how this will proceed. You tell your present self that this is not how your story will continue, and the future you want is a great one. Tell your ex and your thoughts that you are in control, not with words but with action. Take action now and move forward to own your life, to maximize your day to shape your future.

Try this statement of release: *I acknowledge the pain in my life has caused me to make some bad decisions. I acknowledge that I have suffered the consequences of those decisions. I confess that I don't want that lifestyle anymore. I admit I do not want the anger anymore. I admit that bitterness has taken hold of me, and I don't want that poison in my system anymore. I confess that there is no room in my life to house the pain and regret of the past. I declare I am free from the shackles of envy, bitterness, strife, unforgiveness, revenge, and jealousy.*

I declare that my heart is being made pure to love again without fear, to trust again without holding back. I believe that the best is yet to come, and I am making room for all that is pure, good, praiseworthy, freely given, blessed, and lovely to enter into my life.

I am exhaling and letting go of the stress. I am stepping out of my bed without fear or dread. I am hopeful and revived again. Today is filled with possibilities, clues about what is to come; I move forward without fear. I have left an open window to see what I will attract and a clean room to see how I can fill it. When love knocks, I will open, and when the rain falls, I will drink deeply. As the sun rises and everything is exposed, all my flaws, wrinkles, and blemishes, I will proudly gaze and know that I have earned every line. Every scar tells the story of a proud battle fought and won.

It will take time to feel better. Be active in your healing by daily releasing the negative emotions and thoughts. Quickly combat that negative thought by letting it go and in its place encouraging yourself. Don't just release the thought without replacing it, or it will be back. Don't leave space for negative to grow roots and then take over. Speak life-affirming truth to your mind and heart daily.

Look Ahead!

Focus on going forward. There will be changes; there will be distractions. One day you will wake up feeling great about yourself. You will have a plan and take steps in the direction of your goals. You will feel lighter and more hopeful than ever.

You may have even accomplished something on your to-do list, moving you closer to achieving a definite purpose. Then you will get a call or look on your social media page and find out your ex has someone new. They are getting married. You tell yourself I don't care, but your emotions, rising anger, and obsessive investigation of their Facebook page or Instagram feed tell a different story.

Now you have wasted hours and energy chasing your ex's new life, and you are no longer pursuing your own goals. STOP. Refocus. What is the truth in this situation? The truth is, you really do not care about them getting married; if they were single, you would not want them back, so why are you obsessing over this relationship? Could it be that it is not about them? Do you feel beaten by because they were first to find someone new and get into a new relationship?

Whether this relationship works or lasts is not your business. Their new life is not your business, even if you have kids together. Your interest is in ensuring the kids are safe and cared for when with the ex, but the new girlfriend or wife is not your enemy or a target. They are not going to stop you from moving forward and achieving your goals unless you let them.

Don't get off track now; you have just begun to learn about yourself, to explore how to rebuild your life; do not lose hope that your dreams are achievable. When you stop and refocus, eliminating the daily or weekly thoughts about "what is my ex doing now?"

When it is clear by your lack of bringing up their name or questioning your mutual friends, you are getting over them; your ex will notice the change in you, and it will elicit a reaction.

Think back to when they would try to intimidate you with threats, yelling, manipulation, and other ways of instilling fear, insecurity, or doubt. These actions would produce quick and sometimes irrational reactions from the old you. The new you quickly dismiss these temper tantrums, lies, and threats by remembering you are operating in the present, building and working towards a better future. You are no longer susceptible to their attitudes and behaviors; you are a free-minded person.

Post-Divorce

How do I stay hopeful?

Send yourself messages of hope. During this journey, you will need encouragement, and that can come in many forms, letters, and postcards with messages of what you are thankful for, celebrating the milestones in your progression.

Funny milestones you may want to consider: such as month one where you have successfully navigated the repairs in your home on your own; month two, you stop picking up the phone every time the ex calls; month three, you can say their name without curse words in front or after; month four you stop wanting to beat up the lover/mistress; month five you stop stalking their job; month six you stop plotting ways of getting revenge; month seven you hear their voice and do not panic; month eight you drop off the kids without fighting; month nine you stop telling the bill collectors how to find the ex; month ten you pack up the rest of their stuff and give it to them; month eleven you dress up in something beautiful; month twelve you allow yourself an entire weekend of fun out with friends without talking about the ex-once.

Get a good movie, listen to some comedy, do something silly. Meet a friend for lunch and have a good time. Find a reason to smile and keep the smile. Laugh one of those good, lasting belly laughs, and keep on laughing. Taking a moment to breathe will help stop those sudden tears from creeping up on you, and taking the time to be less intense or responsible every moment and allow yourself to be childlike. Practicing being worry-free, if just for a few moments, will be comforting for your soul.

This adult time-out will allow your creativity to flow, your heart to listen, and your soul to exhale the cares and burdens of the day, week, or season. Humans are made requiring recharging; you cannot be refueled with all engines running and moving. There is no on-the-go refueling option; you have to stop, breathe, rest, and allow space and time for the recharging to occur.

Make a list of your favorite things or something fun you want to do in the future. The practice of making a list will help you to feel a sense of joy and positive expectations. It is easy to get wrapped up in the negative because it takes so much energy and focus; therefore, we must train our minds to reset and look positively.

Get outside and into a different place by taking a walk. Don't use the weather as an excuse. Bundle up or dress down depending on the climate and allow yourself to feel the wind, sun, or rain and explore nature. Allow yourself to breathe in the fresh air and breathe out the negative in space like the outdoors, large and expansive, allowing you to feel lighter. Remind yourself there is room to grow, and possibilities exist for something different in life.

Quality Me Time

Every relationship requires quality time to get to know the other person. Carve out quality "me time." Spend it reflecting, capturing the messages you are getting about life. Time to reflect on the people around you and their contributions to your life. What lessons are they teaching you, how they make you feel in their presence?

Time for you to envision the life you want and begin to believe that reaching that goal, that place is possible. We all need a destination, goals to help us get through and find purpose in ordinary day-to-day living.

Reading this book is a part of your in-depth exploration, searching for answers, and understanding. We all long to be known by another person, that knowing involves being understood. To dig deep, find, analyze, and explore the riches inside of you is your task and focus. As you look, examine carefully and ask questions, answers will surface. When those answers surface, it will be your moment of awakening and understanding the why in your what. When you find yourself saying, "how did I get here," the answers will come with quality time spent reflecting on what has transpired previously, what you have been running from up until now.

What seems like nothing is producing moments of learning, self-regulating, and take control of your emotions.

Pursue knowledge from those who have been through a divorce and experienced the unique issues involved. Make friends with someone who can relate to separation and has successfully navigated the waters. Reading this book, you have already taken one step in increasing your awareness of what to expect. You are now able to plan to deal with difficult times. Take in positive messages and begin to build your toolbox of "picking me up to ideas," encourage yourself in the pursuits of your heart. Stay hopeful by having fun and taking time to learn about yourself.

Post-Divorce

Where do I start?

Begin with, answering the question, who are you? If you can't answer the question, start with what is true; your name, age, education level—the simple truth. Then progress to, what do others say about you? I am nice, loyal, kind. Again simple feedback others have given you over the years.

Next, what do you believe about yourself? I believe "others take advantage of me". How can you reframe this? "I am a generous person, and I say yes too easily." Continue with answering the questions what do I believe about myself? For example, "I have a hard time learning new things." The truth is a mix of what you believe, which can be exaggerated by emotions such as fear or doubt. The other half of the mix of what you believe is the reality of what is possible and needed. Below is an example of this activity.

What others say about you	What you believe about yourself	The truth in the middle
You are giving	I give too much, and they take advantage	You are giving and need boundaries
You are bitter	I am angry at the people who left when the divorce happened	You miss having someone reliable to confide in and will work on forgiveness

Learning Your Song

One of the most challenging tasks we face is learning to love ourselves before pursuing a love relationship with another person.

First, develop that relationship with God and self before establishing a relationship with another human being.

Discover what makes you happy, what gets you out of bed in the morning. What scares you, what enrages you, what makes you cry, what causes you to think, react, dance, laugh a deep laugh, or brings you joy. What makes you laugh, moves you forward, inspires you to work hard, and press through tough times.

Everyone has triggers; everyone has needs; what are your needs? We can not expect a partner to come into our lives and know what we want or need. Still, often we don't know what we want because we have not spent the time exploring who we are and asking questions. Yet, we want others and expect others to know.

Below are questions to explore when getting to know yourself.

What I want from others:

Family:

How I need my family to show love?

I feel connected to the family when….

I can give to others….

I want my family to feel…

Friends:

My friendships would be equal if…..

I feel cared for when…..

It is essential for my friends to….

What I need from the others most of all is….

We have the best memories when……….

Co-Workers:

How we divide the work….

Recognition of share investments, sacrifices….

How we help each other….

Standing up for and defending one another….

Communicating needs…...

Intimate partners:

I want in communication when….

This is how to treat my body…...

When we spend time together…...

How we compromise when opinions differ…...

As you answer, these questions get feedback from the people you care about. Be open and prepared that you could hear something you don't like or agree with from them. You cannot ask someone a question when you are not prepared to receive the answer.

If the questions are about how others view you, expect to hear something you disagree with or need to improve. It's your life; you should learn what you want and what you don't want from it. It's your heart; you know what excites it and what does not. It's your body; you should know what works and what does not for you.

This experience will fundamentally change who you are. When your ex leaves, you are forced to acknowledge where you are and what you have left. See the opportunity to evolve into someone else. To move out of your comfort zone and become who you have wanted to be. You have to permit yourself to walk into that new phase of your life.

You have an opportunity to redefine yourself. You are leaving behind arguments, negative thoughts, love that has turned to hate. You are facing the choice of sitting in the dark and being stuck in this place of loss and despair or getting up and turning on the light, cleaning out the room, and taking a deep breath and exhaling the old, embracing the exhilaration that comes with hope, possibilities, and dreaming again. It is refreshing to start over, to leave the baggage behind.

Post-Divorce

How do I deal with loneliness?

There's a big difference between being alone and solitude. You will have times where you feel alone, and that feeling will stir up other emotions, such as feeling unwanted or unloved. When you are feeling lonely, this will cause you to compare yourself to others to ask why? Why do they have someone, and I don't? What's wrong with me? Recognizing this difference between I am alone (having no one to turn to) or experiencing solitude (time to work on myself) is the first step in wresting control of your story.

The Wilderness

Find something beautiful in the desert. Find your time in the wilderness as an opportunity to grow closer to God. When we find ourselves empty, that is when God can come in and fill those spaces. Being left alone for hours at a time with your thoughts can be scary. It can invoke fear, or you can choose to embrace it as an opportunity to get to know the real you. To learn to hear the sound of your voice and the presence of God reassuring, leading, and guiding you.

In the wilderness, you will discover you are changing. You are changing, and it is good. You will notice that conversations may seem different when you are with others, and you will have less to say or find your mind wandering somewhere else. You may find it harder to connect with old friends and become impatient with them. You are changing, and it's okay; let change happen. It is needed and natural. It is time to passionately embrace who you are becoming and freely let others go who cannot grow with you or accept the change.

As you embrace who you have become, you will start to believe that you can reinvent your identity. You will feel a sense of freedom and renewal that was suffocated for so long. This loss has given birth to freedom and a new life filled with possibilities. Don't look back; there is nothing that you are missing that cannot be found as you move forward.

- o   Use the wilderness to experiment with possiblities
- o   Learn to hear your voice
- o   Be willing to change direction and follow peace or power

When the holidays come, Valentine's Day, or your old anniversary date, your emotions may have you tied in a knot. So much so you will be looking for old boyfriends, dates, and acquaintances to occupy your time, so you do not have to feel the loneliness trying to set in. Unfortunately, this will not work because even if being distracted by one of them on this critical day helps, the day after will come. You will still feel the depth of emptiness and loneliness in your mind and heart. You may mask it, but you will not be able to remove it because any man or woman can serve as a distraction, but only the right one can fill that space reserved.

Loneliness can make you compromise and fantasize. Nostalgia can make for a nice fantasy, but the reality is very different. When you become tired of coming home to an empty house, or if you have children arriving home to noise and a to-do list, and you are the honey that has to get it done, the temptation for distraction will grow. As you entertain the possibility of dating again, you will first have to guard against being stuck in the past. The fact of a lousy fit is what you will have to live with when you have settled rather than be honest about your needs.

The right one will settle the question for you, and those feelings of loneliness should not resurface unless you have them in the wrong place in your heart. The desperation for a partner looks like this; during a new encounter with an attractive person, your mind wonders if they are married, and you start to flirt just in case.

So you are sitting there telling yourself that you miss your ex. Ask yourself these questions, do you miss them or the attention? You have the power to overcome the temptation to go backward. It may feel safe, but there is nothing safe about living a life of compromise when it puts the most valuable aspect of your being in danger. You are more valuable than you know; you deserve someone as fully committed to you as you are to them. Your love should be like a valuable prize, not given away like a cheap accessory. Don't get stuck in a pattern of frustration and helplessness when settling for just anyone. Give up the temporary thrill for the long-term happiness awaiting.

Post-Divorce

How do I avoid making a mistake?

Our impulse to measure potential partners' traits and use them to make comparisons among them can lead us to worry that we've sold ourselves short and "settled" for less than we deserve. We shouldn't evaluate potential partners on whether they're good enough and suitable for us.

Consider what "right" in this context means: right for who you are at this time and place in your life. Your vision of the right person will look a lot different when you're in your early twenties and have not yet carved out your place in the world than it does when you're in your forties with much of your life on more solid ground.

You're not going to find the right person by having a long list of potentials and never taking the time to invest. Avoid the mistake of dating too many people, having a standby list, looking around the corner to see if there might be someone else better.

Dating and thinking about remarriage after you have just met only one person may result in the problem of too little information to make a good choice.

Also, consider how you met this person you are considering for a long-term relationship. If you are both recently divorced and recovering, take your time because everyone heals differently. Your timelines for healing will not be the same. When you are thinking of "who is right me?" The first question is, have you explored your likes, dislikes, character. Understanding who you are is vital to know what you want from a partner.

Susan thought, "I dated this man who seemed to be everything I wanted at the time... He was a gentleman, kind, good looking, he opened doors, paid for everything, and treated me like a lady. He was attentive to my needs, and I thought, wow. After five years of being alone, untouched, admired, flirted with but never proposed to for even a date. After so long, I was hungry for touch, love, a good long, long kiss, and even some heavy petting. After being married and sharing a bed nightly with someone, going to an empty bed and house is like leaving a garden full of food and entering a wasteland without water or food. I was hungry."

Hunger for love caused me to confuse lust for love. So when this scenario became clear, I woke to the truth that this person was noncommittal, kind of deciding without saying anything, "he could be a stand-in till Mr. Right comes along." This stand-in was what seemed like the best of both worlds, attention when I needed it and convenience when I didn't. It was the idea of having someone when I was lonely and freedom when I was busy chasing my dreams. I could be single to wait for someone better to come along and in a relationship when I wanted to fend off the riff-raff, who seem to show up like flies. I know love would not settle for part-time, almost, maybe kind of love.

Real love is loving pure and simply, devoted and unhindered. Settling is when we make any one of the following two mistakes:

You might be making the mistake of settling for anyone right now or less than your standard. If you are thinking, *"Where are they coming from and why? Go away, not interested, not settling, not considering. Period. Where is my eagle? Right now, all I see are buzzards, flies, and pigeons. I need to get inspired, and none of what is flying overhead is getting my attention."*

Don't unwillingly give off a sign that says there is a possibility of a relationship if you are settling for less than your standard.

Just for the Release – Letting Go Temporarily

Dear Mr. Right/Ms. Right Now,

Thank you for making me feel desirable, beautiful, and intriguing when I felt unwanted, rejected, and alone. You were my temporary fix to a long-term need, and I am grateful for the memories, touch, and attention. I need to say I am sorry for leading you on; I let my emotions, physical desires, and loneliness lead. I needed time alone to cry, heal, and explore; I grabbed on to you as a drug to escape. I did not mean to lead you on, but my needs cried out loud, and my passions grew hot; my only escape was to yield, and yield I did. I stopped, played, and escaped, but I knew that would not be enough every time I left. I needed more than what you could give, but I could not express it, nor could I work any harder to make you into someone you were not.

You could not have known the standard I was holding you to or the mold I tried to squeeze you into. I apologize not only to you but to myself for allowing the precious gift of intimacy to be given and taken without regard for the hole that it would leave in both of us. I am giving you back your heart to be shared with the mate for whom it is intended. I am taking back my heart, dreams and what remains of my passions and placing them in protective custody until the Right One comes along.

Sincerely,

A Wiser Person.

Mistakes are made when you go backward. Going through old phone numbers: stop digging in the trash. Sometimes you want to hear the words, want to be touched, want someone to talk to, watch a movie with or hold you through the night. Thinking to yourself, *"No sex, just touch...maybe sex but no demands; time, but on your schedule; fun, doing what you want to do. Enjoying convenience but not demanding, on tap when you are thirsty but stopping when you have had enough"*. A friend with benefits, justifying going backward, begins with telling yourself you want a mature, private, no drama, no pain relationship. The truth is all relationships come with baggage.

Mistakes are made when you being to envy someone else's life. There will be days on this journey; you will have to steel yourself to protect your heart and reputation from making foolish decisions that keep you stuck in a mess. The Holidays, New Years', Valentine's Days, and other people's weddings or anniversary celebrations are all opportunities. Opportunities for emotional pain to surface and romantic regret to occur. Seeing the person, you loved with their new partner or wife presents an opportunity for emotional grief.

Post-Divorce

How do I deal with the fear?

Celeste always played life safe; she lived in a townhouse in one of Connecticut's safest neighbors. She drove a small hybrid Toyota Prius and prided herself on making smart and safe decisions. She married a high school sweetheart, thinking she did not have to worry because their families were close. Then the day came that Steven left, and she began a pattern of coming home and sitting still in the dark in her living room, almost comatose most nights. She thought by sitting alone, she could slow down life, and by keeping the lights off, she could escape the reality of what was happening in her life. She was scared, so she hid in her home. *"I'm glad he is gone, but I am scared"* is what she said to herself every night that first month.

After two weeks of not having her calls returned, Celeste's mom visited her and said, "as your mother, I have watched, hoped, and feared for you all your life. I have watched you gain the fairy tale of finding your match and marrying your best friend, the one you loved all these years. As you grew stronger and more confident, I hoped that you would discover who you are; what Celeste wants, likes, and is excited about doing. I hoped you would find your voice and let others know this is you, the grown woman speaking now. The one whose world did not begin and end with her husband, and that you would know your worth. I feared you would look at what was lost and be stuck rather than look forward to what lies ahead. I feared more would be stolen from you than just the years spent with Steven."

Celeste thought to herself the relationship after two years had lost its spark, and she wanted out as much as Steven, but it was safer to be in a relationship than to imagine having to fend on her own. Celeste found her words and admitted to her mother, "mom, I am glad he left, but I'm scared." With that truth spoken, her mother just held her with a firm hug and said reassuringly, "I know, and I will help you through this."

Being scared is part of the process; it is a normal and healthy emotion. Acknowledging the fear and choosing to move forward to achieve your goal is part of the rebuilding. It's like learning to walk. First, it will feel strange, awkward, uncomfortable, and you may fall. As you gain more confidence and learn that falling does not hurt like you imagined it would, it becomes easier; as you get comfortable navigating your way around the room and build strength in your legs, you will notice that you fall less. You will see that you walk quicker, and the movement is leading to progression.

When you find yourself having those days with thoughts of why: Why should I get out of bed this morning? Why should I bother trying? Why make an effort to move on? If you have children know this for sure, your children are watching you. They are taking in what you do and don't do. They are looking to see how you handle this curveball in your life. They are processing when bad things happen; mom lies in bed crying, gets up, makes things better, gets angry, drinks, and ignores us. Mom calls her girlfriends or grandma and then checks out for a while.

Think back to how you saw your mother handle tough times, bad news, or disappointment. Did she fight back, or did she give in? Your children are watching you and rooting for your success. When you have those tough days, remember others are watching, and they want and need you to succeed just as much as you do. You can do this, and you will, despite the fear.

Post-Divorce

How do I stop being anxious?

What about the divorce or being alone causes you fear and distress? What thoughts keep coming up again and again? Anxiety starts with a trigger; this is a thought, followed by changes in your body that signal becoming anxious, uncertain, worried, and fearful. Identify which specific thought leaves you feeling sad, angry, unwanted, hurt, anxious, hungry for affection? Thoughts such as *"why me? Why is this happening? How will I ever recover from this debt? What if I don't get past this like everyone is saying? Who is going to marry someone with all these kids? What are the belief statements you formed as a result of the separation? I fail at everything. I will be alone for the rest of my life. No one wants someone as old as me. Nothing works out right for me."*

Take notice of what happens in your body when these thoughts and questions begin for you. Anxiety symptoms: you feel tired, start sweating, have hot flashes, are light-headed, have shaky hands and legs. Other physical symptoms can be nausea, dry mouth, and restlessness. Your mind starts to race with thoughts, it becomes hard to concentrate, and feelings of fear or dread start to rise.

Breathe – This is important to get your body and mind under control. When anxiety attacks, we stop breathing fully. Leading to shallow, quick breathing makes it hard to regulate the body. Deep breathing gives your body the oxygen it needs to bring the body temperature down and time to control emotions.

Engage in actions that help you to stabilize your blood pressure, slow down your heartbeat and get control of your body. Anxious thinking changes your focus to a negative future.

Get control of your mind focus on the present. Put brakes on the worry by filtering out negative thoughts and outside stimuli. Let the thoughts pass and think about the present possibilities.

Ground yourself in the present by touching, sitting, or holding on to something solid. Grounding helps when you feel lost, overwhelmed, and out of control. The feeling of support by something secure can help you come back to the present in your mind.

Scan your body by sensing where do I feel anxious or stressed in my back, neck, or stomach? Then begin to practice relaxing your muscles after grounding the nervous energy; practice tightening or holding and releasing muscles in your body, starting from top to bottom. Anxiety can be felt by the tightening of the chest or stomach muscles. Practice control tightening and release to gain control of your body and ground yourself.

Anxious thinking changes your focus to a negative future. Get in control by focusing on the present. Worry and stress are created when your focus is on everything that could go wrong. Focusing on the present is more manageable to your mind than an unpredictable future.

You can stop the anxious thoughts and patterns by putting brakes on the worry, filtering out negative thoughts and outside stimuli.

Let the negative thoughts come and go. Don't hold on to the negative thoughts and take a ride on the worry and stress train. Choose to think about the present possibilities instead of the negative future.

If feeling anxious is constant, overwhelming and interfering with your daily life, seek the help of a trained professional counselor. There are some anxious thoughts and feelings you will experience throughout the divorce process. You want to get help if it lasts over two weeks and if it starts to affect several areas of your life or causes difficulty in functioning.

Post-Divorce

How do I forgive?

To forgive your ex; you may have to humanize your ex once again. The need to protect yourself from the pain they caused led to attributing everything wrong to be their fault. Working with your ex if you have children, or forgiving and letting them go entirely, will require making them capable of human errors. This will change your perspective, see the other person's humanity, empathize, and allow them to be capable of mistakes, pain, and weakness. Not to excuse their actions or minimize your pain, but to come to a place of truth and freedom.

In the past, the relationship and break-up have caused a variety of strong emotions. The two of you may have tried to reason with each other, resulting in further disappointment and frustration. The build-up of hurt has turned into anger and distrust; mixed messages from both sides can lead to confusion and further exacerbate feelings of worry and fear.

When you are learning to speak with one another for the sake of children or resolving shared property and assets, it won't be easy. The conversations will be difficult initially because they will be heavily soaked in the past's fresh pain. Practice expressing your thoughts and feelings in a non-confrontational resolution-producing way.

There is no lasting healing without forgiveness. Forgiveness is not quick or easy, but necessary to let yourself move forward. This process begins with forgiving yourself first for every mistake, missed opportunity, or failure.

It is forgiving your ex for every decision, mistake, unmet obligation, or unintended consequence of their actions. There is no time limit for how fast or slow this will take place. You will determine how and when you forgive the other person. There are specific issues and hurts that will take longer and will be easier with time passing. This is because you will change, grow and start a new life making some disappointments of the old life easier to forgive and release.

Forgiveness is also made easier as we humble ourselves with the reminder that we have made mistakes and hurt others in the past. We are capable of disappointing others just as much as your ex disappointed you. You may think I would never do what they have done. This may be true if you are making a direct comparison. If you are answering the question, can I be unfaithful to any promise or fail to keep a promise, and the answer is yes, that reminds you of your humanity.

Everyone has standards, values, and specific rules they would not violate, but can anyone guarantee they will never fail, disappoint, or unintentionally hurt another human being? This is where we are reminded of our humanity, fallibility, and weakness. At this moment, you bring yourself to a level field, and the possibility that you will need forgiveness just as much as your ex needs forgiveness.

Forgiveness does not justify what was done to you; it allows you the room in your heart to heal. It changes the focus from your ex and places the attention back on you and the business of healing from what took place.

The most important person is you and the recovery process; if your energy is focused on the ex, you lose the power, time, and energy needed to heal. Gain back your energy and peace of mind by clearing the clutter and damage made by the other person.

Imagine your mind as having many rooms. The place of unforgiveness as a room in your house full of old, moldy, dirty, broken things and stocked to the ceiling and leaking out of that room is a smell, water, and harmful chemicals that can ruin the whole house. Forgiveness is the act of cleaning out the room, getting rid of all the broken, moldy, old things, and throwing them out of your beautiful home. Getting rid of the mess, chaos, and something that can do more damage to your home the longer they stay, eventfully damaging the whole house.

You can reset and restart by releasing yourself by choosing freely to forgive and choosing to allow yourself access to every room in your mind with peace and confidence. Choosing to build your life and not let others who have hurt you once continue to do it again by holding on to bitterness, anger, and the need for revenge. Through forgiveness, you choose to live free with nothing holding you back, infecting or affecting your life by taking up room needed for trust, love, and living free.

Post-Divorce

How do I stop thinking about revenge?

During this time, you may experience things done to you by your ex that are embarrassing, painful, dehumanizing, or all of the above. There will come a time when you will have to make the hard right choice over the easy feel-good to let them have it an option. Exes are known to use the mistress as a tool to serve court papers to the wife. When a mistress comes up to your door, you may feel emotions that range from rage to shock. For the sake of your future and to avoid possible jail time, you will have to fight the temptation to "beat her ass where she stands." The ex may call you to brag about shopping with the mistress while you and your children worry about how you will eat or pay the mortgage. Exes are known to buy diamonds for the new girlfriend while refusing to pay child support.

You will have to resist the urge to go on social media warfare and let friends or employers know what type of person they are and their double life details. As you read this check-in emotionally, are you angry with the thoughts of all the wrong that inflicted? Thinking of all the ways to get revenge, stop. Stop and remember that there is a reaction to every action; whether or not justified, your decision will have consequences. Consequences that require asking yourself if you are willing to take this fight all the way. And what will you do if it backfires and hurts you or your children more deeply than you planned? The cost of revenge is high, and the constant search for the thing that will make the other person hurt as bad as you feel is unsatisfying.

Revenge is a strong, passionate feeling that snowballs. Suppose you do not take control immediately. In that case, it will go from a small flame to a full-fledged forest fire burning everything in its path quickly and without discrimination, often with innocent victims being harmed in the process. Revenge will overtake the most intelligent person and make them do extremely unreasonable, painful, twisted, and dangerous things.

When the ex does something humiliating, your initial reaction will be to protect your honor. This may come in the form of exposing everything and anything about the other person to make you feel as if you get your integrity back. The very nature of having an ex means that you have lost something. You have lost time and someone you loved to another, and this can cause shame. When you learn that you have failed, the desire to be compensated for your loss as paid back for what was stolen from you, will bring the desire for revenge. Thinking, after all, how dare this person come and take your spouse, someone in whom you invested time, secrets, money, and the best parts of you!

When someone hurts us, it is natural to want to hurt back. Stop the pain and gain mastery over the one inflicting the pain helps us get a sense of control. Losing control and dealing with the fear that this person will try to inflict harm can torment the mind. The need to protect ourselves makes revenge seem like the only way. This person should hurt as I hurt and know that I will not stand for this.

We want them to think twice before attempting to harm us again; revenge brings the possibility of getting that message across.

Before plotting and executing what seems like a great plan, weigh the cost. Think, *"If I do this and it does not go as planned, can I live with the consequences? Can I repair the damage if my actions cause pain, embarrassment, and shame to my family? Will exposing my ex to everyone make him change, will it bring him back, will it break up his new relationship, or will I be left looking like a fool for being with him in the first place?"*

Before you react, go through the checklist:

- Can I live with the consequences of this?
- Who else will I hurt if I do this?
- Will this get me the results I want?
- What do I want from this: satisfaction, remorse, an apology, reconciliation?

You can stop the battle from becoming a war. Choosing not to engage in revenge instead of working on your healing will prevent this from worsening. It will allow you to heal faster and move through the divorce process stronger. Stop thinking about revenge and choose to focus on rebuilding instead. Remind yourself not to stay in the state a moment longer but work every day to get better, stronger, and start living the life you deserve. You have already survived the worst of it, and your best is on the way.

Post-Divorce

How do I stop being triggered?

During this time, you may experience things done to you by your ex that are embarrassing, painful, dehumanizing, or all of the above. There will come a time when you will have to make the hard right choice over the easy feel-good to let them have it an option. Exes are known to use the mistress as a tool to serve court papers to the wife. When a mistress comes up to your door, you may feel emotions that range from rage to shock. For the sake of your future and to avoid possible jail time, you will have to fight the temptation to "beat her ass where she stands." The ex may call you to brag about shopping with the mistress while you and your children worry about how you will eat or pay the mortgage. Exes are known to buy diamonds for the new girlfriend while refusing to pay child support.

You will have to resist the urge to go on social media warfare and let their friends and employer know what type of character they are and the details of their double life. As you read this check-in emotionally, are you angry with the thoughts of all the wrong that inflicted? Thinking of all the ways to get revenge, stop. Stop and remember that there is a reaction to every action; whether or not justified, your decision will have consequences. Consequences that require asking yourself if you are willing to take this fight all the way. And what will you do if it backfires and hurts you or your children more deeply than you planned? The cost of revenge is high, and the constant search for the thing that will make the other person hurt as bad as you feel is unsatisfying.

Revenge is a strong, passionate feeling that is born quickly. Suppose you do not take hold of the reigns immediately. In that case, it will go from a small flame to a full-fledged forest fire burning everything in its path quickly and without discrimination, often with innocent victims being harmed in the process. Revenge will overtake the most intelligent person and make them do extremely unreasonable, painful, twisted, and dangerous things.

The very nature of having an ex means that you have lost something. You have lost time and someone you loved to another, and this can cause shame. When you learn that you have lost to someone else, the desire to be compensated for your loss paid back for what was stolen from you will bring the desire for revenge. After all, how dare this person come and take your husband, someone in whom you invested time, secrets, money, and the best parts of you! When the ex does something to humiliate you, an initial reaction could be to protect your honor and expose everything about the other person while feeling justified.

When someone hurts us, it is natural to want to do the same. Stop the pain and gain mastery over the one inflicting the pain helps give the sense of control. Losing control and dealing with the fear that this person will try again to inflict harm can torment the mind. The need to protect yourself makes revenge seem like the only way. You could be thinking, "this person should hurt as I hurt, and know that I will not stand for this."

Wanting them to think twice before attempting to hurting you again; revenge brings the possibility of getting that message across.

Before plotting and executing what seems like a great plan, weigh the cost. *"If I do this and it does not go as planned, can I live with the consequences? Can I repair the damage if my actions cause pain, embarrassment, and shame to my family? Will exposing my ex to everyone make them change, will it bring them back, will it break up the new relationship, or will I be left looking like a fool for being with them in the first place?"*

Before you react, go through the checklist:

- Can I live with the consequences of this?
- Who else will I hurt if I do this?
- Will this get me the results I want?
- What do I want more war or peace with my ex?
- How will this end: satisfaction, remorse, an apology, reconciliation?

Fight the urge for revenge; it's a trap that many don't get out. These traps can take you for a long, unwanted ride or back and forth with your ex, getting deeper into arguments and conflict. Revenge never works; it is temporary and unsatisfying in the long run. It is an act; the price is high and emotional reward low, the interest can be worst than a lousy loan costing your reputation, freedom, money, and relationship. Forgiveness is a lifetime of peace, building intergrity, and protecting your freedom.

Post-Divorce

How do I protect myself emotionally?

There will come a time where you will have to check yourself and your emotions. Going through this process will test your will, your spirit, and your determination. There are moments, hours, days where you will long for intimacy; the longing will grow until you find yourself willing to make compromises you never imagined. Guard against the feelings trying to convince you to accept or do things not in line with your belief or principles. Learn to feel your body, sense your moods to know when you are most vulnerable, and protect yourself from making a lifetime decision based on hunger, an itch, a desire, or just loneliness.

Have good boundaries. Change your thinking to view boundary lines as safety; they are guidelines that should be followed not to curb but to protect, not oppress, but to contain.

There is always a measure of control, even when things feel beyond your control. Regardless of the circumstances, you always have a choice. You can be locked up in a cell, yet you can be in control, not of the circumstances around you but the emotions, thoughts, and feelings coming out of you. The measure of control lies inside your mind. You control how you react to a situation.

Protecting Yourself in The Beginning

Changing how you interact with your ex can be difficult but will help get your life back on track. The best protection you can have is boundaries, letting your ex know your limits and that you will follow through with consequences when the limits are violated.

Do not answer the phone if it will lead to an argument. You have the right not to be bullied, tormented, or targeted by your ex. Your ex will call and use every opportunity to remind you or failures, to dump their anger on you to make you feel as if it is your fault they picked up and left. You do not have to take this, and you are not the only party in the separation; do not own what is not yours. What is your own, learn, and grow; what is theirs, leave it with them. A bitter person is a dangerous one.

In the beginning, you will have to keep your distance to keep your peace. Guard your privacy; the more information you give, the more that can be used against you. Don't share anything that can be used to hurt you, such as selectively sharing online if your ex has a friend linked to you. Make your life private to keep the ex and other parties out of your business. It will protect your vulnerable heart from any more injury.

Hold on to your honor. Don't fall into the traps of old arguments, debates, and trying to prove something to your ex. It will work out in time, and your self-control will pay off as life takes its course. It is not your job to try and prove them wrong, make them pay, or force respect. Every choice has its consequences; let them happen naturally without interference from you. Therefore, you are not responsible or do not leave yourself open to being hurt whatever the outcome.

When recovering from a loss, you want to be careful not to allow others to manipulate you with threats or fear.

Be tenacious in protecting yourself from verbal threats or manipulation by your ex. Boundaries are not only crucial for your ex but with your children, in particular adult children. Treat your adult children as adults. Remember, you are emotionally vulnerable at this time and may be tempted to cling on to others because you need to feel loved or needed. Create appropriate boundaries so as not to share anything that would harm or conflict with your relationship with your children.

Post-Divorce

How do I trust again?

If you have survived heartache and disappointment, the most difficult thing to do is to trust again. Many of us will open our hearts and our hands. We are targets for others when we believe that people are who they say they are or hoping they will rise to the standard you know they can reach. When this happens for protection, we find ourselves saying, "*I will never trust again. I will continue to be professional but never personal.*" We avoid, hide, resist, or confront, and cut off. Disappointment feels like a sword hurting only at you, yet the person who disappointed you lost out on a gift. In taking the relationship for granted, they have left themselves open for loss. That loss is the gift they were meant to receive in the relationship that was formed. Bouncing back from disappointment will be difficult; it will be painful and take time.

Give yourself that time, but do not make someone innocent pay for what your ex has done; they deserve the best of you. Closing your heart because of the fear of being hurt again, you deny the gift of that relationship. There will always be a risk in a connection; you have to trust that you will heed the warning signs before falling into a familiar trap when it comes.

Being honest about your needs and securities, you can approach new relationships with the confidence that this will not be like your last one. This one will be different because you are different. You have changed as you have recovered from the pain. You have grown wings and become stronger in such a way that you stand taller.

The results of your experiences have made you wiser to the traps of unhealthy relationships. You are more aware of the signs, cautious in your heart, and sharp in your sight to pick up on the potential traps.

The beauty of war is that once it is won, you have learned and faced the unknown. The unknown is now known to you. The things you did not know about yourself or others are now part of your survival tool kit. This war against your heart, the battles for your mind and the struggle for your worth are now over. The lessons taught in the fight for your heart are forever engraved in your mind.

These lessons or battle drills, once rehearsed and lived, become a part of your natural rhythm, and the next time the opportunity to employ the training comes, you will put the lessons to work for you. You will approach what was once tricky, heart-wrenching, or frightening with the confidence of knowing that you can, and you will overcome this challenge.

Nia, 32 years old, realized six months after her divorce that "I'd become accustomed to being alone, and while I wasn't ecstatic 24/7, I was pretty happy. I loved my friends and family (and my kitty!), and I knew I'd be okay if my life stayed the way it was." Mia was content in her new role as a single woman, and where she once dreaded the thought of being alone, she is now embracing what her freedom means. Nia is giving herself time to prepare for the best of what God has to offer while taking the time to enjoy herself, using this opportunity to grow, live, laugh, and then love again.

Don't jump into a new relationship or make any rash decisions; your feelings will become clear as you become clear. Jumping into a new relationship too soon leaves you open and vulnerable to ending up with a jerk in disguise. This person seems nice initially and then a few months later starts to reveal himself, being rude to others, angry all the time, living off others, making comments about your body or what you need to work on, on edge constantly. This type of person makes you ask, *"am I addicted to dysfunctional relationships? Is this someone I want to spend another day with, never mind the rest of my life?"* Save yourself the trouble, headaches, and potential expense of having to change your phone number; run away from these types.

Each time we say goodbye, we grow stronger. Saying goodbye allows you to know that you are not stuck, dependent, or lacking if that person or thing no longer exists in your life. Saying goodbye removes and frees you from what has held you back, moving you forward and making room for the good that wants to come into your life. Learn to love new things, new opportunities, new people, and new adventures; new days all hold possibilities, mysteries, and potential. What will make the new beneficial depends on what you draw from it. Work on yourself, and love will find you.

Post-Divorce

How do I avoid repeating relationship mistakes?

Moving forward involves knowing what you want from a relationship. Once you have identified what you want, it is essential to ask for it and clarify. As women, we are more likely to not ask for what we want and then not get it, but stay in a compromised relationship longer than we should. We are reluctant to ask for our needs for several reasons, including the fear of being vulnerable, not trusting others, not being clear in what we want. The step of asking for what you want is one in many ways to help communicate your expectations and desires.

When asking for what you want, it is essential to acknowledge that you deserve the best and have a right to have what you need. You do not have to settle for less than you deserve or want; having this firmly planted in your heart will help you ask for what you want and stick to it until you get that very thing. The more specific you are and simple in stating your request, the greater the likelihood of getting what you have requested.

Identify the attributes you are looking for in a relationship before deciding whether or not this is what you want. A person may have some of what you are looking for while lacking in some other areas. It is important to be clear about what you want.

Here are some attributes you might look for:

- Empathetic, Loving
- Emotionally Satisfying, Committed
- Affectionate, Respectful

- Open-Hearted, Honest
- Tender, Caring, Kind
- Understanding, Humorous, Fulfilling
- Appreciative, Thoughtful, Fun
- Forgiving, Consistent
- Sexually and Emotionally Faithful
- Intelligent, Nurturing
- Interesting, Pleasurable, Generous
- Willing to share the Housework
- Responsible, Hardworking
- Financially Stable, Sharing
- Communicative, Trusting, Affectionate, Safe

Treat the above list as a guide, not a ruler, for measuring your potential mate. This is to help you think about what is attractive to you in a partner. Once you answered what you need from someone, it is easier to know when you have found it. Clarity will also allow you to sort through what you will or will not accept. Be straightforward and clear about your needs, communicate and be confident why.

Post-Divorce

How did I lose a spouse and pick up a habit?

Coping with divorce will first look like picking up a habit. Some habits can develop into an addiction if not careful. You may ask why is there a chapter on addiction in a book on divorce? This chapter is necessary because when dealing with intense loss, pain, and loneliness, you are more susceptible to increased drinking, medication misuse for sleep, or engaging in life-controlling behaviors. According to the American Society of Addiction Medicine, "Addiction is characterized by an inability to abstain consistently, impairment in behavioral control, craving, diminished recognition of significant problems with one's behaviors and interpersonal relationships, and a dysfunctional emotional response."

Divorce can be traumatic and stressful, adding to the vulnerability level for forming a harmful habit or practice. The occasional glass of wine with dinner turns into a bottle of wine daily or alcohol mixed with other substances. A warning because the consequences of developing habits are high. Alcohol or drugs will impact your ability to bounce back or thrive while going through a divorce.

If the substance is a normal part of your dinner routine or weekend experiences, consider cutting down or stopping altogether as a protective measure. If this gives you anxiety, it may be time to get a professional evaluation to determine if drinking or substance use has become a problem.

You have a lot at stake, and substances can become a dangerous mix when you are at a low emotional point, exhausted, and looking for ways to cope. Even if you are not a regular drinker, the one bad day you are under the influence and send an intoxicated text message can lead to trouble. If you get into a physical altercation with your ex-spouse because of being drunk, this can cause legal or financial consequences. One incident of DUI can change or impact a custody battle significantly. When going through a divorce, especially if it's contentious, your behaviors and habits will be under a microscope if things are not favorable for the other party. Don't give your ex-spouse information, incidents to be used against you in any way.

Monitor any habits that have slowly crept into your life and examine if it has grown out of control. If you are spending $100 a day or week on excessive shopping, drinking, gambling, drugs, or anything that alters your state of mind or provides an escape from dealing with life, take a look at the habit.

- Is it causing problems in other areas of your life?
- Are friends and family concerned it is out of control?
- Are you worried about it affecting your mental or physical health?
- Is it interfering with work or a relationship with your children?
- Are you becoming more and more isolated to engage in this activity or habit?

Yes to one or more of these questions can become an indicator of a possible problem developing. Seek professional help to determine if the behavior is forming a dependence and help to stop engagement in psychological or physically harmful behaviors. Addiction begins with abuse or misuse of a substance and, over time, can develop into dependence.

Post-Divorce

Will my finances recover?

Yes, they will; little by little, your finances can recover the relationship and income loss with discipline and a plan. It will mean sacrifices have to be made to get there. The sacrifices made now will pay off later with less debt and more financial security. The financial debt will cost you more than just money; it takes away your peace of money, steals your time, and borrows on your tomorrow. When all your bills are paid, there is a great sense of satisfaction that is exhilarating. It is like having a constant stream of fresh, crisp air flowing through every vein and a feeling of weightlessness.

Conquering debt frees you from fear of creditors or not balancing the financial load, the fear of embarrassment, shame, and loss of property. To reach the place of economic freedom, you have to take some simple but tough, steps beginning with an honest evaluation of your spending habits and motivations, when you spend the most, and why you are spending.

Some of the excuses for "why" of spending are "I don't have anyone to buy me nice things," "I work hard and deserve it," "it's a treat," "shopping helps me think and escape," "its girl time with my friends." Most people spend more money when they feel lonely, bored, unappealing, or need retail therapy. Advertisers tell us to pay to have a better lifestyle, feel good, measure up to others, and be someone else. We will even spend money to save, i.e., purchasing in bulk things we will never use or need, driving out of the way to save on gas.

Tackle the root of the overspending problem and work out a plan to change your habits. Financial decisions are based more on emotion than logic. Stop the self-sabotage by understanding your weaknesses and know your triggers. If you have been under emotional stress, it can lead to overspending. Shopping can offer stress relief, and even if money is the source of stress, spending more can be a way to cope with worries about finances because, for that moment, you are in control and telling yourself that you deserve it.

Financial survival requires getting a spending plan and sticking to your goals. Staying out of your favorite stores, not going shopping with a friend because they need a buddy, not giving away money to others who think you are their banker. To reach your goal and stay on track, it will mean saying no to yourself and others when it comes to spending.

We live in a society where we want everything, and we want it now, without considering its future impact. This attitude is learned from a young age where kids want things immediately, and parents give in. However, delaying immediate gratification impacts our success, both financially and in all aspects of life. Becoming debt-free is possible if done with a plan, enforced with discipline, and guarded by a commitment to a greater goal.

Post-Divorce

Will the kids/family forgive me?

Divorce, separation, and abandonment are challenging to process in private; when public is can be devasting to everyone involved. If the divorce involved violence, aired publicly online, or made known to all co-workers and friends, the consequences are higher. The circumstances, the publicity, and the results may have been difficult and embarrassing, yet never forget that everything is repairable. The repairs will not remove scars, yet mending will take place. Your relationship with your children may not look the same, but it can become more profound if you are willing.

Some of your children may not speak to you, but you can always talk to them. You can write notes, letters and speak from your heart, not your head; do not try and make your former spouse or partner look bad or place blame. Focus on what you love and miss about your child and share it with them. They may not write back or acknowledge they have read your letter, but human curiosity will bring them to a point where they will find themselves reading it.

Two of the common feelings that will surface in several areas of your life are guilt and inadequacy. Guilt can come from not seeing children, family, or ex-family members. Inadequacy feelings can come from comparison. One myth that will lead you to compare is below.

Myth: They will like the new partner or spouse more than me

Children are more intelligent than we give them credit for, and at all ages, they see and sense more than they share or can put into words.

You are their parent and will always hold that special place in their hearts, mind, and spirit. No one can ever really separate a child from their parents; even parents who have made terrible choices or have not always been there throughout their childhood and into adulthood command a place in the hearts of their children. Therefore if your children have to be around the new partner or spouse, allow them to form their relationship with that person, so you cannot be accused of turning the children against them.

Remember, there is a difference between position and title. Your children calling them mom/dad or stepmom/stepdad is a temporary position when applied to anyone but you. Mom/Dad, when applied to your role, is a permanent title and a sacred place in the heart. Your children will bestow on you the title; no one can ever replace you or take that from you. Others can hold the position, but they will never hold the title because the connection is not biological; it must be shaped, nurtured, and grown. Title and position are two different things. Children have an incredible capacity to love; they can love you and other significant adults in their lives. Reduce your child's stress and anxiety level by allowing them to care about and love others without being made to choose sides or feel guilty.

If you have said things in the past about the other person or your ex-spouse, choose to change how you engage today. Decide to let a comment or action go by weighing if it is essential or not and considering the consequences.

How you react or respond will determine what lessons and cues your children learn from you. Do not use the kids as pawns between you and the ex. Do you want your children to know you as well adjusted, single happy person or a bitter, miserable ex/divorcee? When you are with your children, focus on them and your relationship; choose not to engage with or acknowledge the partner because they are inconsequential in your life. As long as your children are safe, unharmed, and cared for, your ex's new partner does not matter in your new life.

Post-Divorce

Am I too old to start again?

This is a myth. We can find many reasons to disqualify ourselves from a good life. You may think you are too old, or you have too many kids to have another relationship. Your age or the number of children you have will not deal with starting another relationship.

For middle-aged men and women, you may have been in a long-term relationship lasting over several decades, and now you think, what now? If all you can think of is "I wasted all those years," now is the time to realize you have more in your favor, thanks to all those years. The time is not lost; it was invested; now it's time to make a new investment. The investment is in you. Do not let the next 20 or 30 years suffer at the expense of the last 20 or 30 years. You deserve more; do not fear the unknown because, at one time, you were at the beginning place you are now. The ex is history, and now you are about to make room for the present, the current, and the future. Fearing what you don't know is normal, but before you reject the possibilities, stop, entertain the "what if," ask yourself, "why not." Why not me, and why not now live a new chapter and love differently. The goal is not to recreate the past with someone new. The goal is to create something new with someone new.

If you are worried because you have several children, they will also embrace your children when the right person falls in love with you. Let them know at the beginning that you are a package deal, and then they can choose to accept, love, and embrace the kids, the good parts, and the challenges.

You want someone in it for the long haul, the good, bad, and the complex; a mature person preferably has children they care for and have a healthy relationship.

If they do not have a healthy relationship with their children, be very careful. If their children do not like or respect them, take heed. Children know who we are; they know the secrets, the things chosen not to be shared with potential partners. They have seen their parents at their worst and best, often holding a mirror to the truth, being careful to watch, listen, and evaluate to keep themselves from being surprised. When dating with children, remember: everyone desires to believe, trust, and we are all susceptible to allowing others to fool us. Be careful that your desire to pursue love does not lead you to pretend and believe things that are not true. Trust your instincts and listen to the concerns of your children when choosing a mate.

Post-Divorce

How can I tell if things are getting better?

As you go through the healing process, some mindsets and ways of thinking will point you toward success and other thinking traps that will cause you to struggle. You want to make decisions towards a healthy mindset to succeed in the divorce recovery process. Below is a listing of emotions and actions taken when in a positive mindset.

- Feeling Positive, you will increase in Optimistic thinking
- Self-motivated, you are building a track record of commitment
- Taking responsibility for how you feel and making improvements
- Creating opportunities by remaining flexible and taking the risk
- Creative and allowing yourself to see it by trying new things
- Willing to ask questions and seek answers
- Tenacity by staying committed to getting healthy

If you are reading this and thinking, "I am not there yet, still struggling with the divorce." Do not worry or become anxious; give yourself grace and time. Reading this book was the first stage of awareness, and change will come as you think differently.

A significant life event has just occurred; it is expected you will struggle with the meaning. Daily remind yourself this will take time to adjust. Be aware when you are in the emotional state of struggle or feeling stuck. The goal is to identify the emotion and change it. We don't want to let a negative emotion grow and grow. Working to change the feeling to a positive one or keep it from growing is key to feeling better long term.

Post-Divorce

What's next for me?

You may be asking yourself, what is next? How does this story end? Where do I go from here? From here, you get to choose. You choose how your story continues in this new chapter with the choices you make today and every day. It's time to get off the ropes, be like a professional boxer, stop taking the punches, and come out swinging. You were born with the strength to fight, and now is your turn to fight back, to move forward and swing back. Swinging not to hurt someone, swinging back to let everyone around you know that you are back in the fight, in the game, and you came to win. You will stand firm; you were quiet and reactive before, but now you will be heard and proactive with your future.

We all would like a peek around the corner to know what is coming next and how it will happen. Curiosity, anticipation mixed with fear leading to daydreaming and playing out possible scenarios of our endings. You get to choose now, even if you did not get to choose then. The story as it is written is not the ending, just the plot for now. You have weathered this storm as you will weather any in the future. You can, and you will make it with your mind, your peace, and you are worth intact. You are God's beloved and, therefore, worthy of love.

You are worth having someone fight for you, believe in you, and stand by you. You are worth being pursued, being loved, and your affections are worth earning as well as your intimacy worth cherishing.

The possibilities await, the dream can be realized; you have been one for beating the odds, no time like now, no situation better than this one to test your resiliency and your fortitude. Go and win, move forward, and shake things up just by being yourself.

About the Author Page

Gessy Martinez is the author of several books, an award-winning public speaker and trainer, mother, licensed minister, Business and Personal Development Coach, and Licensed Professional Counselor. She blends skills in management, supervising, planning, development, and experience as a parent of young adults, teen and school-age children, and President of Aspire and Reach for More, LLC. She is familiar with struggle and passionate about helping others through encouragement, training, and counseling.

To connect with her, visit the website: aspireandreachformore.com

If you enjoyed this book, I would love to hear your thoughts about it! Stop by Amazon and leave a review, or Facebook and leave a message.

Other books by this author

- The Weekend Entrepreneur
- The Mommy Entrepreneur
- 52 Reasons to Live: Why Greatness Refuses to Die
- Why Strong Women Struggle: Win the Battle in Your Private, Professional, and Spiritual Life